Tantra–Mantra–Yantra in Dance

An Exposition of Kathaka

New Vistas in Indian Performing Arts

1. **Hindustānī Music and the Aesthetic Concept of Form**; by Anjali Mittal (ISBN 978-81-246-0134-1)
2. **Hindustani Sangeet and a Philosopher of Art:** Music, Rhythm and Kathak Dance *vis-à-vis* Aesthetics of Susanne K. Langer; by S.K. Saxena (ISBN 978-81-246-0180-8)
3. **Speaking of Dance:** The Indian Critique; by Mandakranta Bose (ISBN 978-81-246-0172-3)
4. **Performing Artistes in Ancient India**; by Iravati (ISBN 978-81-246-0207-2)
5. **Ritual as Ideology:** Text and Context in Teyyam; by T.V. Chandran (ISBN 978-81-246-0275-1)
7. **Hindustani Music:** A Tradition in Transition; by Deepak Raja (ISBN 978-81-246-0320-8) (Hb); (ISBN 978-81-246-0321-5) (Pb)
8. **The Art of Tabalā Rhythm:** Essential, Tradition and Creativity; by Sudhir Kumar Saxena (ISBN 978-81-246-0368-0)
9. **Kathaka, The Tradition:** Fusion and Diffusion; by Ranjana Srivastava (ISBN 978-81-246-0473-1)
10. **Elements of Hindustani Classical Music**; by Shruti Jauhari (ISBN 978-81-246-0568-4) (Hb); (ISBN 978-81-246-0569-1) (Pb)
11. **Khayāla Vocalism:** Continuity within Change; by Deepak Raja (ISBN 978-81-246-0481-6) (Hb); (ISBN 978-81-246-0482-3) (Pb)

New Vistas in Indian Performing Arts, no. 6

Tantra–Mantra–Yantra in Dance

An Exposition of Kathaka

by

Ranjana Srivastava

PRINTWORLD

Publishers of Indian Traditions

Cataloging in Publication Data — DK
[Courtesy: D.K. Agencies (P) Ltd. <docinfo@dkagencies.com>]

Srivastava, Ranjana, 1948-
Tantra–mantra–yantra in dance: an exposition of Kathaka / by Ranjana Srivastava.
(New vistas in Indian performing arts, no. 6).
p. 25 cm.
Includes passages in Sanskrit (roman).
Includes bibliographical references (p.)
Includes index.
ISBN 13: 9788124602683

1. Kathak (Dance). 2. Art, Tantric. 3. Yantras in art. 4. Mantras in art I. Title. II. New vistas in Indian performing arts, no. 6.

DDC 700.482 21

ISBN 13: 978-81-246-0268-3
First Published in India in 2004
Second impression, 2014

Printed and published by :
D.K. Printworld (P) Ltd.
Regd. office : *Vedaśrī*, F-395, Sudarshan Park
(Metro Station: Ramesh Nagar)
New Delhi - 110 015
Phones : (011) 2545 3975, 2546 6019; *Fax*: (011) 2546 5926
e-mail : indology@dkprintworld.com
Web : www.dkprintworld.com

dedicated in feet of

My Guru's
Vikram Singh Ji

who taught me my first step in dance

and

Prem Lata Sharma
my Guru in Śāstra

As a mark of my affection and sense of
deep gratitude

Preface

LIKE all Indian arts, the Indian classical art form of dance *Kathaka* — the classical dance of north India — is sublime, philosophical, esoteric and divine. From the mundane to the transcendent, from the human body to beyond the physical form, from religion and aesthetics to metaphysics, the journey is not a simple linear growth, but rather a whole process of evolution and revelation in which one has to loose one's self in order to experience the ultimate joy/truth, *Saccidānanda. Nāda-sādhanā* by the *yogī*s and *svara-sādhanā* by the *sādhaka*s of *saṅgīta* is an important aspect of the spiritual discipline and culture of India, where *Saṅgīta* is also referred to as *Nāda-yoga*. It is, in fact, the process of the understanding and the realization of the inter-relatedness and the interdependence of the Indian arts. It is in this process that dance expands to embrace the other disciplines of Yoga, viz., Tantra, Mantra and Yantra.

My inspiration to write a book on *Tantra-Mantra-Yantra in Dance : An Exposition of Kathaka* is largely a result of my growth and evolution as a student, artist, performer, teacher, and researcher of *Kathaka* dance, as well as my effort to integrate the traditional knowledge which I received from my late *Guru*, Vikram Singhji, largely in the form of an oral tradition, combined with a critical approach in an academic context after I completed my Ph.D. on Kathaka : Its Origin and Development (A Study based on Ancient and Mediaeval Sculptures and Paintings) under the supervision of Dr. T.K. Biswas, Jt. Director & Administrative Head, Bharat Kala Bhavan, BHU. My association with Prof. Prem Lata Sharma, Vice-Chairman,

Sangeet Natak Akademi and Prof. Ranganayiki Ayyangar, Dept. of Musicology, BHU, further sharpened my questioning instincts. The book is also, perhaps partly, a reaction to the gross commercialization of *Kathaka* both by the dancers as well as those in charge of preserving and promoting the Indian classical dances as a heritage.

Indian classical dance, *Kathaka,* is part of a vibrant living tradition, a cultural heritage of India. As part of a living tradition, *Kathaka* has constantly been evolving. I am witness to this process of evolution and growth for almost fifty years! As an art form *Kathaka* is a product of human organizational skills, aesthetic sensitivity and cultural enterprise. Besides, dance as a timeless art, as *yoga,* is perhaps only an elaboration of a coherent cosmic system, which helps transform the knowledge of principle into practice. The *guru-śiṣya paramparā* was, in fact, the embodiment of such a tradition in which values and principles were bequeathed as a legacy from one generation to the other. In the words of Stella Kramrische, "Tradition thus is not only an oral transmission of information and beliefs from ancestors to posterity but also an inherited culture. It is a body of doctrine and discipline, put forth and revealed in the words of the Veda." (vide Exploring India's Sacred Art). The Veda teaches the means for the realization of a state which ultimately yields abiding satisfaction to man. According to it, it may be found in *Brahman, Nāda, Bhūman* or *Amṛta*. The Veda also emphatically states that man can never realize the object of the innermost yearning of his heart, what is *Alpa* or *Martya* in the Vedic terminology. Thus, *saṅgīta* (music and dance) to be Upavedic or Vedic as a *summum bonum,* must partake of the character of *Brahman, Nāda, Bhūman* or *Amṛta*. The *Chāndogya Upaniṣad* (1.24.1), defines *Bhūman* and *Alpa* as "Where a man does not see another, does not hear another, does not know another, there is Bhūman, and where he sees another, hears another, knows another, there is 'Alpa' that which is Bhūman is immortal and that which is Alpa is mortal." According to *Brahmasūtra* (1.3.8), this *Bhūman* is *Parā Vāk,*

beyond the *Paśyanti.* The *Bhūman* or *Parā Vāk,* thus implies, extraordinary concentration on the *Ātman* or *Paramātman,* which can only be made possible in an esoteric process, and *saṅgīta* appears to be best suited and fitted as an instrument for use or employment in that process, for the reasons that it is the most tangible and the least utilitarian of all arts and it thus enables the human mind, more than any other art, to detach itself from worldly affairs and to engage itself in the contemplation of the Divine (vide *Saṅgītarāja,* ed. Prem Lata Sharma).

Another characteristic of Vedic *Brahman, Nāda, Bhūman* or *Amṛta* is that it is *Saccidānanda.* The Vedic philosophy postulates that of the three aspects of *Saccidānanda, Cit* is superior to *Sat* and *Ānanda* is superior to *Cit.* Of the four Upavedas, *Gandharva* is considered pre-eminent, as it is derived from the *Ānanda Aṁśa* of *Saccidānanda;* the *Dhanurveda* and *Sthāpatya* or *Arthaśāstra* are initially concerned with the gross matter (*mahābhūtas*) and are thus derived from the *Sat Aṁśa.* The science or art of *Āyurveda* is derived from the *Cit Aṁśa* of *Saccidānanda* as it deals initially with *Prāṇa* which is nearer to *Bhūman* or *Saccidānanda* than is the gross matter of *Dhanur* or *Sthāpatya* Upavedas. *Gāndharvaveda* deals initially with sound (a *Tanmātra*) which is more close to *Nāda-Brahman* Himself.

The *Parā Vāk* or *Nāda,* in order to be seen, heard and known, must have a body or form. *Nāda* must have a *Tanu.* The R.V.S. II, mentions the body of *Nāda* :

सुस्वरवर्णविशेष रूपं रागस्य बोधकं द्वेधा।
नादात्मं देवमयं तत्क्रमतोऽनेकमेवाउच।।[1]

Indian dance, if performed as a ritual, sustains a continuity both emotional as well as experiential, thus practise leading to meditation, which ultimately helps man to unravel the secrets of nature. The path is arduous and perilous because

1. Vide, Mahārāṇā Kumbhā; *Saṅgītarāja* vol. I, ed. Prem Lata Sharma, see Sec. III, Topical Notes, "Bhūman" as the Ideal of Saṅgītaśāstra and its application for secular music, p. 71.

the journey is from the profane to the sacred, from illusion to reality, from man to divinity. There is in the process a complete metamorphoses in form, function and behaviour.

In the fast changing cultural scenario, with the doors and windows widely opened towards globalization, with a consumer-oriented approach, there has been an acute turn towards commercialization. In fact, with the advent of satellite television, there has been a revolutionary change in our methods of entertainment and education as well. It is perhaps only the aspect of *artha* (money) which seems to be fully validated. The horizon of *Kathaka* dance today, is wider than ever before. With an unprecedented increase in the number of dancers all vying for commercial success, the spectrum is much more colourful, the repertoire is, perhaps, much more secular with the presentation of new items and themes in works of fusion and choreography, the desire of the dancers for greater self-expression, bold enough to enunciate revolutionary trends; an effort to re-choreograph with a mixture of the old and the new, indigenous as well as foreign. Though the efforts are applaudable, yet I feel that somewhere and at some point, we are loosing out on the centuries old spiritual base/aspect of the dance form. What was this spirituality and what was the element of sentient ? In what way did it manifest in dance? *Kathaka* especially.

It is true that in the due course of time, with the decline in Sanskrit and the Hindu culture, the cultural graph of the subcontinent also started to show a decline. The spiritual base and cause of Indian art and culture receded into the background against the emergence of a mosaic culture in which both the indigenous and the exotic elements were to be represented. The Persians, Moguls, Britishers could never grasp and appreciate the true value and significance of the Vedas and thus also the arts derived from the Vedas. In the *Nirukta* (8.2-3, 9.16) there is a specific mention of a *Kāthakya Ācārya*, who is meditating upon *Nārāsaṁśī*. During the course of my Research I felt ever so poignantly that a dent had been made in the tradition of *Kathaka,* which showed generic similarities with *Dhrupad Nṛtya* ! But then each generation must adopt and adapt the continuity being maintained in and through the modes of transmission, practise and meditation.

It was only after centuries of development and growth that *Kathaka* dance evolved and attained a beautiful form. Not that in those thousands of years there was no fusion, diffusion and confusion, yet, in spite of all the impacts and upheavals, as a result of the various historical, social, cultural and geographical factors, in spite of the vanishing wealth and splendour of temples, courts and palaces of ancient and mediaeval India, dance still remained a *sādhanā.* Today, as we move on into the twenty-first century, a new millennium, I feel that we have eroded our spiritual base in the name of modernity and popularity. I have been grappling for answers to these and many more questions. All books on *saṅgīta* refer to the importance of the human body, they contain chapters devoted to the *piṇḍotpatti. Saṅgītaratnākara* clearly states that the purpose of dealing with the human body is because of the four types of physical bodies; (those born from sweat such as a louse, those born from sprout such as creeper, those born from the womb such as human being, and those born from egg such as birds), the human body is most suitable for the manifestation of *Nāda-Saṅgītaratnākara* (1.2.16-17). The *Bṛhaddeśī* (1.11.18) clearly states that there is no *gīta* (song, music) without *Nāda,* there are no *svara*s (musical notes) without *Nāda,* there is no *nṛtta* (dance) without *Nāda,* hence the world is of the essence of *Nāda. Nāda* has been the subject of study by philosophers, musicians, and tāntrics. The *Saṅgītaratnākara* (1.3.6) states that *Nāda* composed of the syllables *Na,* representing vital force and *Da* representing fire, is produced by the interaction of the two. As *Nāda-Brahman,* it is worshipped and it manifests the phenomenon of the universe. Yet the million dollar question remained — What was its relationship with dance ? Another question related to the aforesaid one which always vexed me was : when dance exploits the human body most fully and completely, then why does it constitute the third and last part of the *trika* of *saṅgīta* ? What is the significance ? Though much work has been done on the vocal aspect of *saṅgīta,* dance strangely seems to have been somewhat neglected.

My main object was to explore the possibilities of interpreting *Kathaka* in terms of a sacred art. Much has been talked about the secular aspect of *Kathaka* in which it was held as a medium of mere entertainment, especially in the courts of the Muslim rulers and the Nawābs of Oudh, or even when *Kathaka* was referred to as *nautch* during the period of British rule in India. It was my firm belief and conviction that if the origins of *Kathaka* were ingrained in the system of the Hindu arts, an exhaustive analysis of its movements and sound patterns would very definitely lay bare the profundity of thought which went into the making of ancient Indian traditional arts and thus reveal the sacredness of the art of *Kathaka* Dance. To some extent, the objective was achieved in my Ph.D. thesis, Kathaka: Its Origin and Development (A Study based on Ancient & Mediaeval Sculptures and Paintings).

Also the concepts of space, time and sound are not arbitrary inventions but correspond to certain irreversible cosmic principles. Their manifestation in the Indian arts, whether architecture, painting or dancing is fundamental and cannot be altered or their function be inter-changed. The lines : vertical, horizontal, oblique, curved or spiral, all have their natural, specific and intrinsic meaning and character and the patterns which result from their varied interrelation and interaction have a far-reaching and profound effect in terms of visual reactions, psychological and spiritual association in the beholder, as Boner rightly says :

> Their meaning is grasped intuitively because the human personality is of one order with the forms of the universe

> and responds spontaneously to their elemental aspects. . . . The figural compositions refer to mysteries, spiritual events, descent of divine forces into the cosmos. It is left to the artist to translate and interpret the mystery of the cosmos into the mystery of artistic forms.

The lines and the circles, the dots and the triangles, thus made a bid to point towards some kind of a tāntric impact upon our art of dancing. India records a strong historical root of such a tradition, and its impact could not be ruled out. The theological and the mystical intermingling for a more harmonic integrity between man and nature bestowed the symbolic representation of the universe or the symbols with powers of the cosmos, which were crystallized within them. The question remained : How did it make an impact upon *Kathaka* ? Or to put it differently, in which way did *Kathaka* absorb the sacred knowledge within its form, though the form has been evolving and thus changing over the centuries.

The book is an effort to re-discover the lost meaning, which, it seems was much more deeper and of a much more exclusive nature than realized in recent times. No such study can lay claim to perfection, simply because there are many levels and points of reference. The imagery and the symbolism involved, also has many aspects and levels. There is and always has been a great interplay between the forces of nature on the one hand and the traditional and intuitive awareness of the artist on the other hand. Besides, tradition is always being re-interpreted in the name of growth and evolution. The process of re-interpretation and re-integration many a times has led to the extinction of one form and the re-birth of another form. *Kathaka* as a classical dance of north India is well known to everybody, but the generic relation of *Kathaka* with *Dhrupad Nṛtya* is camouflaged. Though *Dhrupad* as a style of singing has become rare, *Dhrupad Nṛtya* is extinct. The *Dhrupad* singers even today refer to the spiritual and metaphysical levels in their vocal renditions. Was *Dhrupad Nṛtya* also influenced in a similar way ? In which way did *Kathaka* carry forward the convictions and the meanings of the magnetic culture of the sub-continent of India.

The book presents four chapters, supplemented with photographs, and a conclusion :

Chapter I : Tantra — Discusses Tantra and its approximation and application to Dance; Chapter II: Mantra — Deals with the aspect of sound and its manifestation in Dance — *Kathaka;* Chapter III: Yantra — Explores the techniques of *Kathaka* which create distinct *yantra* formations both in the physical movements of the dancer in the surrounding space as well as on the dancing floor; and Conclusion.

This book is a small effort in understanding and exploring the roots of our dance *Kathaka.* In the following pages I would like to share the revelations when a dancer becomes a *sādhaka* and dance becomes a *sādhanā* for the experience of *Saccidānanda.*

I would like to express my deep gratitude to Dr. T.K. Biswas, Jt. Director and Administrative Head, Bharat Kala Bhavan, BHU, Vārāṇasī, for his help whenever I needed it. He was kind enough to go through my manuscript and suggest corrections. I would also like to thank Dr. T.N. Misra, Curator, Bharat Kala Bhavan for giving me moral strength when at times I was dejected. I would also like to remember and express my sincere feelings for late Prof. Premlata Sharma, Vice President, Sangeet Natak Akademi, New Delhi. She was my beacon in the field of *śāstra.*

I would especially like to thank all the staff of Bharat Kala Bhavan, in the Library and the Painting Section for their help. My thanks are also due to Dr. S. Chopra, Senior Curator Painting Section, and Sri Ramachandra Singh and Sri P. Prakash Rao, for their efforts in helping me to get good photographs for my work. My thanks are also due to the Library and staff of the Parsvanatha Jain Institute Library, Vārāṇasī. Sri A.K. Mishra needs special thanks for the typing of the manuscript in record time. My family has always been a source of my

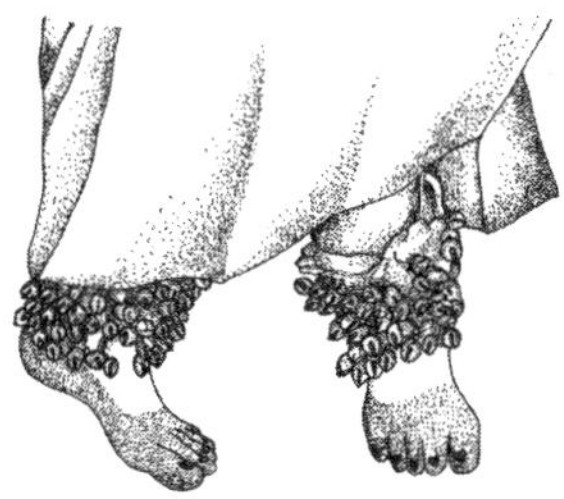

strength and I take this opportunity to thank my husband and my children for all their love. I would also like to thank my parents for all their love and hard work, in my years of training to become a dancer. I am very much grateful to Mr. Utsav Sharma for designing the cover. Last though not the least I would also like to thank my publisher, Sri Susheel K. Mittal of D.K. Printworld, Delhi for his ready acceptance to publish my work.

Contents

Key to Transliteration

अ *a* (but)	आ *ā* (palm)	इ *i* (it)
ई *ī* (beet)	उ *u* (put)	ऊ *ū* (pool)
ऋ *ṛ* (rhythm)	ए *e* (play)	ऐ *ai* (high)
ओ *o* (toe)	औ *au* (loud)	अं *ṁ* (*saṁskṛti*)
अः *ḥ* (*prātaḥ*)		
क *ka* (skate)[1]	ख* *kha* (blockhead)[1]	ग *ga* (gate)[1]
घ *gha* (loghut)[1]	ङ *ṅa* (sing)[1]	
च *ca* (chunk)[2]	छ* *cha* (catch him)[2]	ज *ja* (john)[2]
झ *jha* (hedgehog)[2]	ञ *ña* (bunch)[2]	
ट *ṭa* (start)[3]	ठ* *ṭha* (anthill)[3]	ड *ḍa* (dart)[3]
ढ* *ḍha* (godhead)[3]	ण* *ṇa* (under)[3]	
त *ta* (path)[4]	थ *tha* (thunder)[4]	द *da* (that)[4]
ध* *dha* (breathe)[4]	न *na* (numb)[4]	
प *pa* (spin)[5]	फ* *pha* (loophole)[5]	ब *ba* (bin)[5]
भ *bha* (abhor)[5]	म *ma* (much)[5]	
य *ya* (young)	र *ra* (drama)	ल *la* (luck)
व *va* (vile)	श *śa* (shove)	ष *ṣa* (bushel)
स *sa* (so)	ह *ha* (hum)	क्ष *kṣa* (*kṣatriya*)
त्र *tra* (*trishūl*)	ज्ञ *jña* (*jñāni*)	

°*ṁ* *anusvāra* (nasalisation of preceding vowel)

: *ḥ* *visarga* (aspiration of preceding vowel)

* No exact English equivalents for these letters.

[1] guttural [2] palatal [3] lingual [4] dental [5] labial

List of Illustrations

1

Tantra

INDIAN culture is deeply rooted in religious thoughts and Indian religion is a part of Indian *darśana* (philosophy).[1] In the great cycle of life and time, religion is sought as a means of salvation from the profound joys and miseries of life. The cultural history of India reveals an insatiable thirst for the Absolute — the Unknown. The significance of this socio-religious-cultural tradition is an important factor in the study of the spiritual base of the Indian tradition of *saṅgīta,* i.e., music (vocal and instrumental) and dance.[2] The subcontinent of India has always attracted people from all over the world; whether they came as invaders, plunderers, tourists, merchants or students, there was a spirit to accommodate all. What was this spirit, and how did it work? This spirit was the religious spirit based on the eternal fundamental values of *satya, yajña* and *tapas* (truth, ritual and penance). This religious spirit was perhaps only an urge for setting spiritual values, of a very systematically defined cosmic conception and a transcendent metaphysical vision,

---

1. From the moment of conception to birth and death, the Vedic tradition refers to *śoḍaṣa saṁskāra*s. Also see Prem Lata Sharma, "Sadhana Ke Samartha Upaye Ke Rupa me Saṅgīta" (Hindi) Article published in *The Alchemy of Love and Wisdom*, ed. and comp. U. Sharma, Radha Publications, New Delhi, 2002, pp. 112-17.
2. Śāraṅgadeva, *Saṅgītaratnākara* vol. I, 1.1.21, Sanskrit Text and English translation by R.K. Shringey and Prem Lata Sharma, Munshiram Manoharlal Publishers, New Delhi, 1999, p. 10.

in action, for India has always been, basically, a spiritualistic country and its people the lovers of spirituality and spiritualism. This religious spirit however, should not be confused with the pursuit of religion.

All Indian art, according to Coomarswamy, is an expression or a statement of racial experience,

> it has an intelligible meaning and a definite purpose. . . The meaning is embodied in its spiritual values, principles and thoughts, which have been bequeathed after thousands of years of penance and practise, and the purpose is effective communication of those spiritual values, principles and thoughts which are based in the eternal truth and which could help to develop an ideal man and society both. . . . Love for art was known by love for/of life.[3]

According to the *Taittīriyopaniṣad,*[4] the individual soul is identical with the universal soul in the solar orb. Blessed with innumerable faculties, the individual soul (*jīva*), which is a part of the universal soul, thus becomes a very powerful medium in unravelling the secrets and the mysteries of the universe which have always fascinated and charmed his imagination.[5] Thus, the various disciplines, *śāstras*, in the field of religion, philosophy, fine arts, *saṅgīta* and others are, in fact, man's efforts towards removing the veil of ignorance (*māyā* or *avidyā*) for a better and a more fuller understanding of the eternal truth, in order to experience the eternal bliss — *Ānanda*. It is for this reason that the

3. A. Coomarswamy, *Fundamentals of Indian Art*, The Historical Research Documentation Programme, Jaipur, 1985, See Ch. on Introduction to Indian Art.
4. *Taittirīyopaniṣad*, 3.10.4.
5. C. Sivaramamurti, *Approach to Nature in Indian Art and Thought*, Kanak Pub., New Delhi, 1980, See Foreword by Rai Krishnadasa, where he says : "it is the actual participation of nature and the resultant human involvement which matters in Indian Art and poetry."

human body has been consecrated in the Hindu culture, as in the systems of *Haṭha Yoga* and *Rāja Yoga* which start with the human body and the human mind.[6] In fact, the system of Tantra or *Tāntric sādhanā* is entirely based on the cardinal belief that the truth is to be realized in and through the human body. In fact, all yogic practises like *mudrā, āsana, prāṇāyāma,* etc., which are important constituents of any *sādhanā,* Vedic or Tāntric and more specifically, for our purpose *saṅgītika,* are basically methods of preparing the human body or the *jīva,* in which resides the soul, not only to apprehend but also to experience the Absolute as *Saccidānanda* (truth-consciousness and bliss).

The origin of the word Tantra is from the Sanskrit root *tan,* which means "to spread" or "to expand." Some scholars have also traced the origin to *tatrī* or *tantrī,* which means to originate or to know. The two roots *tan* and *tantrī* have also been used in the sense of "spreading" or "weaving." The other meanings of "Tantra" as described in lexicons are : *siddhānta* (conclusion); *śrutiśākhā* (a branch of *śruti,* i.e., the Vedas); *itikartavyatā* (set of duties), *prabandha* (composition); *śāstraviśeṣa* (a particular *śāstra*). Some scholars also derive Tantra from *tanu* (body). Tantra when denoting a kind of *śāstra,* stands for a set of doctrines, practises mystic syllables, metaphysical speculations, magic, etc.[7] In its present and widely accepted sense today, Tantra means a special kind of yogic *kriyā,* which helps in understanding the profound concepts and questions of life and also helps in achieving and realizing the profound

6. T.N. Mishra, *Yoga-Tantra and Sensuousness in Art,* D.K. Printworld, New Delhi, 2003, Ch. 2 Kāya Sādhanā, wherein the writer refers to other kinds of *yoga* such as *Mantra Yoga, Laya Yoga, Bhāvanā Yoga* and *Sahaja Yoga. Yoga* involves psycho-physiological processes.
7. S.C. Banerji, *A Brief History of Tantra Literature,* Naya Prokash, Calcutta, 1988, see Introduction.

experiences through the human body, with the aid of mystic diagrams (*yantras*) and mystic sounds and words possessing esoteric meaning (*mantras*) (see *Pls.* 1, 2). It also has its own special *śāstra* (literature) and it finally helps in attaining salvation. Tantra is both an experience of life as well as a scientific way by which man can bring out his inherent spiritual power and for this reason tāntric rituals form the basis for many religious and philosophical systems in India such as Śaiva, Śākta, Jaina, Buddhist and Vaiṣṇava.[8]

The tāntric way gives supreme importance to the *deha* or *kāya* (the human body) and very categorically admits that the mysteries of the universe may be sought in the body itself. The tāntric view regards the world as a macrocosm, *brahmāṇḍa* and the body as a microcosm (*kṣudra brahmāṇḍa).* It is made up of the same five elements, fire, air, water, earth and ether, which also constitute the universe. Both are known as *piṇḍa* or *bhāṇḍa*. The body thus becomes not just a means or a vehicle for the realization of the Supreme through proper practise of *sādhanā,* but in the course acquires qualities which raise it far above the level of ordinary human beings. This is, in fact, a process of transference of energy which is only possible through the process of inner visualization, which again can only be made possible through meditation that involves a whole process of yogic *kriyās*. This process/practise of visualization and meditation is the same in religion and art,[9] because there is a certain similarity of purpose, the

8. A. Mukherji, *Tantra Art — Its Philosophy & Physics*, Ravi Kumar, New Delhi, 1971, p. 11. Also see Sri Shankar Bagawatipada, *Saundarya Lahari, the Ocean of Beauty,* Theosophical Pub. House, Madras, 1965. It states in the translation "The worship of Viṣṇu, Śiva, Śakti and other Vedic deities have been elaborated by the large number of Āgamas, Tantras, Purāṇas Itihāsa, all within the ambit of the Vedic ideal."

same eagerness to bring forward a central idea : "the power of the cosmic forces, the eternal presence of the deity mark the artistic rendering of the Dance of Śiva, of Viṣṇu's three steps or of his Cosmic slumber. . . ."[10] (see *Pls.* 3, 6).

Boner explains, that such a vivid grasp of the significant movements, or such a sensuous and powerful treatment of form or even such delicate inflections of feelings and their expressions was only possible because of the artists' complete control over his personality, which we may call *yoga* as well as his profound knowledge of nature, which we may call meditation.

> The traditional artist was dedicated to the realization of a metaphysical or religious idea and not the realization of his own personality. The rules according to which he worked were not arbitrary or conventional, but were derived from spiritual conceptions which were broad and comprehensive enough to allow him to work in the fire and freedom of his own inner vision. Where everything grows out of and is controlled by the same principle, there is no difference between law and freedom.[11]

The different religious, philosophical or metaphysical

9. A. Mukherji, *Tantra Art — Its Philosophy & Physics*, p. 13, wherein it is stated "According to Coomarswamy: "The practise of visualization, referred to by Śukrācārya is identical in worship and in art. The worshipper recites the *dhyāna mantra,* describing the deity, and forms a corresponding mental picture, and it is then to this imagined form that his prayers are addressed and offerings made. The artist follows identical prescriptions, but proceeds to represent the mental picture in a visible form, by drawing or moulding." It would do well to remember the "Citrasūtra" of *V. Dh.* 3.35, 5-7, wherein it is clearly stated : *yathā nṛtte tathā citre."*

10. Alice Boner, *Principles of Composition in Hindu Sculpture, Cave Temple Period,* Leiden. E.J. Brill, Netherlands, 1962, see Preface.

11. *Ibid.,* p. 36.

systems, whether Vedic or Tāntric, advocate injunctions, *niyama* and practices, *vidhi,* in the physical, vital and mental planes by which an individual is able to attain the two-fold end upliftment or progress, *abhyudaya* and renunciation in the sense of supreme realization of freedom, *niḥśreyas* by laying stress on the principle of purification, *śodhana* or *śuddhi,* and upliftment, *uddhāra,* leading to the unification with the Absolute.[12] Ingrained in the metaphysics of Veda, Yoga and Tantra, the system of *saṅgīta,* finds inspiration in the all-pervading Nature, *Prakṛti. Prakṛti* in Tantra is identified with the female energy or Śakti and is inseparable from Śiva who is pure consciousness. The two are inseparable and may be understood as the static or dynamic or the negative and dynamic aspects. The *tattva* (element) of Śiva and Śakti lies within the human body. Śiva resides in the highest plexus (*sahasrāra*) which is in the cerebral region while Śakti resides in the lowest plexus (*mūlādhāra*) and *sādhanā* consists in raising the Śakti from the lowest plexus in an upward movement till she becomes united with Śiva. The right side of the body is believed to be the region of Śiva and the left side, that of Śakti. This is also the tāntric conception of Ardhanārīśvara[13] (see *Pl.* 7). The creative union of Śiva and Śakti is *nāda* and the seed that issues

12. T.N. Mishra, *Impact of Tantra in Religion & Art, op. cit.*

13. *Ibid.*, also see C. Sivaramamurti, *Nataraja in Art Thought and Literature*, Publications Division, Ministry of Information and Broadcasting, Govt. of India, 1994, p. 85, wherein there is a reference to *Nṛtta Ratanāvalī* 1.2 : "Śambhu, who as Ardhanārīśvara has his beloved spouse engulfed in his body, carefully watches through his glances the movements of his hands in their appropriate position, as he holds to his left the delicate *lāsya,* beautified by the glory of gesticulation of emotions, the other half, to the right, the rhythm of the more powerful *tāṇḍava* to the deep note of the *ḍamaru* hand drum," also see p. 84, where he says that Śiva alone is capable of *lāsya* and *kaiśiki vṛtti* (more the sphere of women) because Śiva alone is eternally Ardhanārīśvara. Also see →

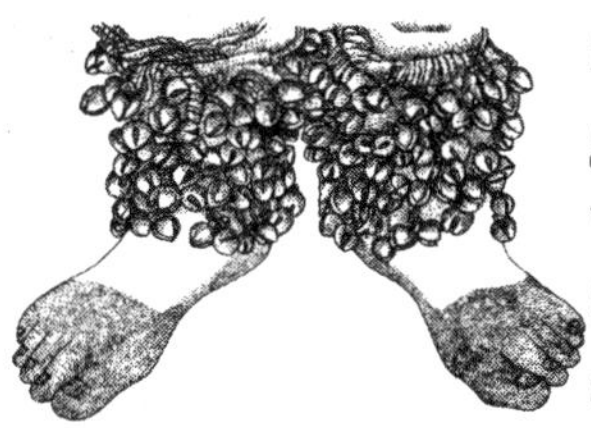

from the union is *bindu.*[14] The *bindu* is also called the *ghanībhūta bindu,* i.e., it is pregnant with all those elements which constitute the totality of Manifestation. The *Saṅgītaratnākara* refers to it as the *brahmagranthī.* It is significant that *Nāṭya Śāstra* (4.255.256) clearly mentions that after seeing Śiva's dance with *recaka* and *aṅgahāra*s, an *uddhata prayoga* (vigorous and energetic) Pārvatī also danced. It was a *sukumāra prayoga* (soft and gentle)[15]— a clear reference to two *prayoktā*s (performers), exhibiting two different kinds/forms of energy, yet complimenting each

→ *Aparājitaprcchā, A Critical Study* (Encyclopaedic Manual on Art and Architecture), Lal Mani Dubey, Laksmi Pal, Allahabad, 1987, p. 301, where, in the reference to *Liṅga Purāṇa,* it is stated that the Ardhanārīśvara form is the composite of *liṅga* (represented by Śiva) and *yoni* (represented by Pārvatī), their union creates the world. This perhaps is symbolical of the synthesis of the two creeds of Śaivism and Śāktism. Ardhanārīśvara also symbolizes the blending of *Brahman* and *māyā.*

14. A. Mukherji, *Tantra Art — Its Philosophy and Physics, op. cit.,* wherein he says, that "All movement has its origin and consummation in *bindu* or point-limit," the invisible central point of a *yantra,* which has existence but no magnitude; for magnitude proceeds from the feminine power (*śakti*) or *bindu.* All creation according to Tantra is preceded by a focal tension. *Bindu* carries within itself the seeds of its future, its multiple potentialities, symbolically represented by the white and red points. He also says that there is no place in the phenomenal world where the one *bindu* will not be found. So *bindu* is the ultimate point of power beyond which a thing or energy cannot be contracted or condensed. It is both the nucleus of matter (*jara*) as well as the nucleus of radiant consciousness (*caitanya*). *Bindu* contains within itself the two poles (zero and infinity) and all that lies in between. But for actual creative process *bindu* must evolve beyond duality to the *trikoṇa,* the triangle, the first rectilinear figure to define dimension. pp. 27-28.

15. Bharata Muni, *Nāṭya-Śāstra,* 4.256, with commentaries *Abhinavabhāratī Madhusūdanī* and *Bālakrīḍā,* BHU, Varanasi, 1971, p. 396.

other. It was a beautiful expression of the tāntric vision of the *kuṇḍalinī* awakening and moving in an upward movement for unification with the eternal *tattva* Śiva, in the *saharsrāra.*

> Śiva is the Yogeśvara, who remains in eternal *samādhi* or in union with himself. The whole universe is created by the Śakti of Śiva. Śiva as a dancer performs the *tāṇḍava,* His Śakti, Pārvatī, performs the *lāsya* in delicate rhythm. Both are relative quiverings of the same power or Śakti, one in the male and the other in the female form; or the one in the macrocosm and the other in the microcosm. . . . Both Śiva and Pārvatī watch the dance steps of each other. These are both valid vibrations according to modern science, but the spiritual demonstrations of a hidden power according to metaphysics. Perhaps in world symbolism, there is nothing so inspiring and deeply pregnant with meaning as the idea of the dance of Śiva, typifying the eternal rhythm and polarity at the root of the infinite creative process[16] (see *Pl.* 3, *Pl.* 7).

Interestingly all Hindu arts trace their origin in some divine being.[17] The *Aparājitapṛcchā* clearly states that the universe, earth, *vāstu, dharma,* the arts and sciences have a divine

16. V.S. Agarval, *Śiva Mahadeva — The Great God* (*An exposition of the symbolism of Śiva*), Prithvi Prakashan, Varanasi 2nd edn., 1984.

    In the Vaiṣṇava tradition, however, Kṛṣṇa and Rādhā are the two manifestations of the One Supreme Reality.

17. Śiva is known as Naṭarāja, the Lord of dancers, the creator of *karaṇas* and *aṅgahāras*, basic units of dance (*NS* 4.13, tr. *Madusūdanī-Bālakrīḍā,* p. 232); Kṛṣṇa is known as Naṭavara, the first/leader of dancers. Kṛṣṇa was an incarnation of Viṣṇu, Himself a great dancer who used beautiful *aṅgahāras* in his fight with the demons, Madhu and Kaiṭabha (*V.Dh.* 24.9, ed. Priyabala Shah, Oriental Institute Baroda, 1958, p. 124). It was from Him that Brahmā was inspired to create *vṛttis* in *nāṭya* (C. Sivaramamurti, *Nataraja in Art Thought and Literature,* infra, p. 261, "So Viṣṇu also as the *ācārya* of *nāṭya* has shown His great importance in relation to the →

origin and are created by the divine will.[18] The *Viṣṇudharamottara Purāṇa* also refers to the divine origin of the arts. In fact, the traditional Indian view stresses that the divine wisdom is the supreme illuminor and the ultimate source of all forms, either manifest or unmanifest. All art forms are, in fact, a manifestation of a systematically defined cosmic and transcendental vision and experience. The enormous body of *saṅgīta śāstra* thus contains numerous references to the religious practices and life of its people because the entire scope and purpose of the *śāstra* is the realization of the four principles/goals of life : *dharma* (religion/duty); *artha* (money/meaning); *kāma* (sex/desire); *mokṣa* (freedom/liberation).[19] Abhinavagupta himself ascertains that the 36 chapters of the *Bharatasaṁhitā*, are devised on the 36 fundamental elements of the *Tantra-*

→ *vṛttis*." The graceful movements of the limbs of Viṣṇu as He fought Madhu and Kaiṭabha gave rise to Kaiśikī and other *vṛttis*). Similarly, Pārvatī is credited with the *sukumāra prayoga* in dance which she later taught to the ladies of Saurashtra Dwārakā. *S.R.* 7.5-7, ed. Subrahmanya Sastri, Adyar Library and Research Centre, Madras, p. 3; Sarasvatī is also referred to as Vāgadevī. Also see Prem Lata Sharma, *The Alchemy of Love and Wisdom*, p. 112, infra., in which is published "Sādhanā ke Samartha Upaye Ke Rupa me Saṅgīta" (Hindi), wherein she says that the gods and goddesses are not only fond of music but in their ultimate form they are *nādātmaka*.

18. *Aparājitapṛcchā — A Critical study*, Encyclopaedic Manual on Art and Architecture, compiled by Bhuvanadevacarya, tr. Lal Mani Dubey, Laksmi, Allahabad, 1987.

19. *Saṅgītaratnākara* 1.1.30, p. 11, refers to music as a means of realizing the four primary values of human life, viz., righteousness (*dharma*), wealth (*artha*), enjoyment (*kāma*), and emancipation (*mokṣa*). Also see Prem Lata Sharma, *The Alchemy of Love and Wisdom*, *op. cit.*, p. 113, wherein she says that the *sādhanā* of *saṅgīta* may be done at various levels; *dharma, artha, kāma* are realized at its lowest level, while *mokṣa* is realized at its highest level.

Śāstra.[20] *Nāṭya-Śāstra* (4.328) states that those who sing and dance the *caritas* (description of the deeds and action in poetry/songs) of Śiva will be emancipated and thus reach *Śiva-loka.*[21] In fact, all the gods and goddesses of the Hindu pantheon are associated with some instrument either as their attribute or as their *āyudha* (weapon). *Saṅgītaratnākara* also refers to instruments related to *devapujā.*[22] The tradition of *rāga-dhyānas* makes a specific bid at pointing towards a very close relationship between music (vocal/instrumental) and *sādhanā.* This tradition was, perhaps, started with the *upāsanā paddhati* (worship/ritual) and it reveals the impact of Tantra, while about the sixteenth century AD, a very dominant note of *nāyaka-nāyikā bheda* in different conditions of *śṛṅgāra* (*saṁyoga, viyoga,* etc.) also becomes visible.[23] The depictions of *rāgas/rāginīs,* as *devatās* or as *nāyaka/nāyikās,* sometimes suggestively or at times prominently reveals them to be standing, sitting in some static or dynamic (i.e., which shows a strong movement) dance posture (see *Pls.* 8 & 9). The dancing figures depicted in Ellorā (eighth century AD approx.), Khajurāho (ninth-eleventh century AD approx.) and Koṇārk (thirteenth century AD approx.) show a strong influence of Tantra on sculpture.[24] *Nāṭya-Śāstra,* equates *raṅga-pūjana* to a *yajña,* i.e., the worship of the stage is like a ritual and when performed well, will bestow on the worshipper (in our case actors/directors and dancers) the desired boon.[25] Sivaramamurti states,

---

20. *Nāṭya-Śāstra* with commentaries *Abhinavabhāratī, Madhasūdanī, Bālkrīḍā,* infra., pp. 5 and 587.
21. *Ibid.,* 4.328, p. 493.
22. *Saṅgītaratnākara,* 6.768; 6.1097, 6.1125, vide Prem Lata Sharma, *The Alchemy of Love and Wisdom,* infra, pp. 110-12.
23. Prem Lata Sharma, *The Alchemy of Love and Wisdom,* infra., p. 111.
24. S.C. Banerjee, *A Brief History of Tantra Literature,* Naya Prokash Calcutta, 1988, p. 138.

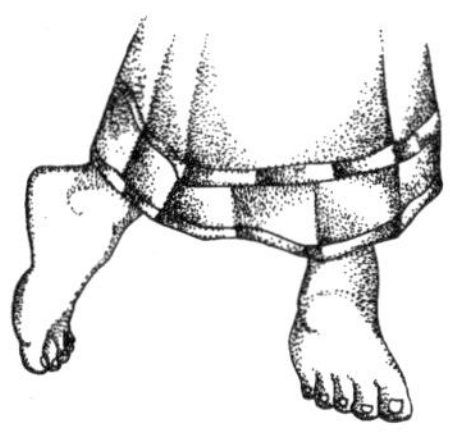

Nāṭya has been considered in India to be one of the most ancient forms of language for worship, where both *mantra* and *tantra* are used. *Mantra* is utterance, and *tantra*, symbolic gesture. It has thus found great favour with religion and ritual all over the country. The great celestials have been associated with it. In fact a thanks offering is given to them in the *raṅgapūjā* where Śiva, Devī, Viṣṇu, Brahmā, Sarasvatī, Kārttikeya, Indra, Dikpālas, Mātṛkās are all mentioned. The Mātṛkās are not merely Mātṛkās, but dancing Mātṛkās. They are called Nāṭyamātāraka (see *Pl.* 10).

The Indian arts of music and dance, *saṅgīta,* work simultaneously on two levels: the material or the worldly and the spiritual or the metaphysical, because the avowed purpose is the search and realization of the Absolute Bliss, *Saccidānanda.* It was precisely for this purpose that the noble art of *nāṭya* (drama), the fifth Veda, the *Nāṭyaveda,* was created by Brahmā to live an ideal life on the path of righteousness, prosperity, fame and liberation. Thus, *nāṭya* became an imitation of the quintessence of the three worlds.[26] *Saṅgīta,* thus formed an integral part of the major scenes of ritual and festivity. *Saṅgīta* thus became a *sādhanā* (a term basically used for religious practice), an unfolding

---

25. *Nāṭya-Śāstra* : 1.127-130; infra, p. 153. The *yajña* is performed with the utterance of *mantras*. Also see C. Sivaramamurti, *Nataraja in Art Thought and Literature,* infra, p. 8, wherein he says : "The highest tribute to *nāṭya* has been paid by Kālidāsa, who describes it as a pleasant ocular sacrifice for the gods, as the sages consider it. Rudra has rendered it into two modes, the violent and the soft, in his body intermingled with that of Umā. In this, every act in the world, arising from the three-fold natural disposition and suggestive of varying moods is well represented. Dance alone in different ways is the one thing that pleases alike people of varied tastes . . ." and again "Dance is not only a pleasant ocular sacrifice but it is also a popular adjunct to a regular sacrifice itself," p. 20, same book.

26. *Ibid.,* 14-17, pp. 50-56.

of the power of the self (*ātmaśakti*), brought about by self-realization (*ātmadarśana*). All *sādhanā* in same form is *yoga* (i.e., disciplining of the body physical, mental and spiritual for various purposes). This also includes the process of meditation. Patañjali lays the principles of *Aṣṭāṅga Yoga*, because through *yoga* the individual achieves integration, first within himself and then between him and nature. In fact, part of *tantra-sādhanā* deals with *yoga*.[27] Sivaramamurti elaborates the same thought, — Dance as a symbol of creation (an aspect of *yoga*) is represented in the concept of Ardhanārīśvara, and Viṣṇu dancing as Mohinī is the symbol of existence and sustenance (see *Pl.* 7). Ardhanārīśvara is the union of *prakṛti* and *puruṣa* in the sense that *jñāna* (knowledge) and *jñeya* (the known) are together. There can be no *jñāna* without contact with *jñeya* and *jñeya* cannot exist apart from *jñāna* that comprehends it, so they both complement each other. It is in the same sense that Kālidāsa has said that *vāc* and *artha*, utterance and its sense in union

---

27. D.N. Bose, Haldhar, Hiralal : *Tantras (Their Philosophy and Occult Secrets)*, V.K. Publishing House, New Delhi, 1981, p. 131, wherein he says : "Yoga conveys the idea of union or addition but in a special sense it means withdrawal of mind from everything and concentrating it upon a particular object or Deity. It is that psychic condition which enables one to be in closer communion with the Deity. It is in fact the science of union of human being with the Divine dwelling within him. It is the sum of physical, psychical and mental processes which bring about deep transformation of human being, an awakening in him of the new man which is unattainable by a man in his normal state. It awakens new modes of consciousness, new perceptive faculties, new power and potentialities that exist in the sub-conscious region . . . the use of which quite transforms the delicate complex of which we are made. For this utmost self-control, a strict moral and intellectual discipline are necessary." Also see Prem Lata Sharma, *The Alchemy of Love*, . . infra; p. 117, and T.N. Mishra, *Yoga Tantra and Sensuousness in Art*, D.K. Printworld, New Delhi, 2003, p. 56.

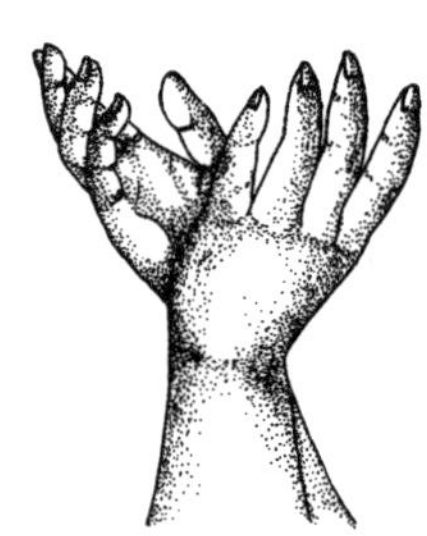

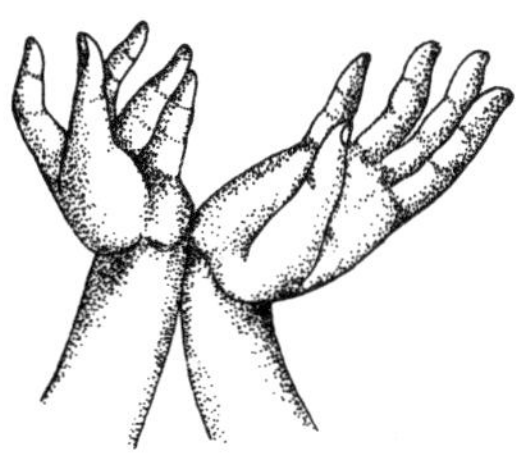

are Śiva and Pārvatī as Ardhanārīśvara. Thus, *lāsya* and *tāṇḍava* do complement each other in *nṛtta*. He further says that *pramāṇa* and *prameya* in śāstric terminology are the very essence of the concept of Ardhanārīśvara.[28]

Discipline (*anuśāsana*) is strictly advocated by the *gurus* in the process of learning *saṅgīta*. According to Bharata, this very clearly falls in the three stages of learning: *grahaṇa* (practise), *dhāraṇā* (assimilation), *jñāna* (meditation).[29] This third stage leads to creation and ends up in liberation, a stage where there are no bindings or fetters. The entire knowledge acquired over the years becomes internalized, thus becoming one with the inner consciousness. The entire process or *prakriyā*, which leads artists/*sādhaka*s into achieving this non-dual (*sahaja*) state is the process of *sādhanā*. This state in the *Tantra-Śāstra* is known as the *turīya* state, which is a very high state. The *sahasarāra cakra* is supposed to contain a field of knowledge which is known as the *turīya*, and in our highest experience is self-revealed.[30] In dance, the author feels that, perhaps, this process explains the technique of "fusion." Caution should however be made : fusion when done by people who have not reached the last stage reveals "confusion," but the same when done by a *sādhaka* develops or creates new art forms, or novelty in the already existing art forms.

Along with discipline-devotion and faith are also important factors in the training/learning process of *saṅgīta* which exhibits proximity with religion. The *maṅgalācaraṇa śloka*s in the books on *saṅgīta* provide a glimpse into this element of devotion and faith.[31] Indian dance includes

---

28. C. Sivaramamurti, *Nataraja in Art Thought and Literature*, p. 25, infra.
29. *Natya-Śāstra*, 1.21-22, p. 72, infra.
30. T.N. Mishra, *Impact of Tantra in Religion & Art*, infra.

music and thus it becomes the highest form of yogic activity:

yajñasya phalam aśnute.

The offering of dance to the accompaniment of vocal and instrumental music assure the merit of a sacrifice performed:

mokṣopāyam cha vindati.

It not only fulfils all desires, but assures liberation (*mokṣa*) for the devotee or *sādhaka.*

dhanyam yaśasyam āyuṣyam svargolokapradam tathā īśvarāṇām vilāsam tad ārtānam duḥkhanāśanam mugadhānām upadeśam tat strīṇām saubhāgyavardhanam śāntikam pauṣṭikam kāmyam vāsudevena nirmitam

— *V-Dh.* 3.34, 30-31

It particularly pleases Viṣṇu who created the art, that assures wealth and fame, prolongs life, cheers the dejected, admonishes the blunder head, enhances feminine grace, promises auspiciousness and prosperity, here and hereafter.

puṣpanaivedyadānebhyo nṛttadānam viśiṣyate

---

31. Prem Lata Sharma, *The Alchemy of Love and Wisdom, op. cit.*, p. 120, wherein the scholar says that glimpses of *bhakti*, in *saṅgīta śāstra*, may be seen in the *maṅgalācaraṇa pada*s or the *udāharaṇa pada*s. The *maṅgalācaraṇa pada*s may be seen starting from Abhinavagupta's *Abhinavabhāratī* and the later books keep in line with this tradition. According to the scholar, the tradition/*paramparā* of *udāharaṇa pada*s begins with the *Nāṭya-Śāstra* and its expansion may be seen in the *Bharata-bhāṣya* by Nānyādeva, and in the *Mānasollāsa* by Someśvara. *Saṅgītaratnākara* by Śāraṅgadeva is largely a repetition of the *udahāraṇa pada*s of Nānyādeva. All these examples are devoted to Śiva, while those of the *Mānasollāsa* are devoted to Viṣṇu. The fifteenth-century, *Saṅgitarāja* by Mahārāṇa Kumbhā contains many, *udahāraṇa pada*s, many of which are new, but they are all devoted to Śiva. In some of the books of the seventeenth century AD, such as those of Bhāvabhaṭṭa, one of the topics is *Devastuti*.

> The offering of dance is considered higher than all other offerings like flowers, oblations, etc.[32]

Thus, the aspiration to achieve the *sahaja* (non-dual) state in search of the Absolute Bliss (*ānanda*), through the human body, led to the development of various systems of education : the *Tantra-Śāstra*, the *Saṅgīta-Śāstra* and more specifically, to our point of reference, the *Nṛtta-Śāstra* as codified in the *Nṛtta-Sūtra*.[33] This *Nṛtta-Sūtra* is a codification of all the knowledge from the various fields and disciplines which in spite of having their own autonomy are interrelated and interdependent. It is for this reason that in the Indian system there is a reference to 64 *kalās*. The streams of Indian culture, religion and philosophy are so reciprocally entwined that it is almost impossible to separate one from the other. For this reason many a times we find universality of thoughts, ideas and words, yet with a difference ! For instance, *nāda, bindu* and *mudrā* are words which are profusely used in the *Tantra-Śāstra* : *nāda* stands for the flowing state of energy and *bindu* its concentrate form. In music (vocal-instrumental) *nāda* could perhaps be understood as the open sound and *bindu* as the sound produced with a closed month; viz., *mudrita gamaka*.[34] Extending the ambit of *nāda* to dance, the *Bṛhaddeśī* clearly states ". . . there is no *nṛtta* (dance) without *nāda,* hence the world is the essence of *nāda* (18)"[35] and "from *nāda* is formed

---

32. Vide C. Sivaramamurti, *Nataraja in Art Thought and Literature, op. cit.*, p. 11.
33. Ref. to the Ślālin & Kṛśāsva *Nṛtta Sūtras* by Pāṇini, though no work belonging to them has yet come to light. .

    Nṛtta-Sūtra of *V. Dh.*, III *Khaṇḍa* under *Citra-sūtram*.
34. Mātaṅga Muni, *Bṛhaddeśī*, vol. II, ed. Prem Lata Sharma and A. Beohar, IGNCA, Motilal Banarsidass, Delhi, 1994, p. 320.
35. *Ibid.*, vol. I, 2.18, pp. 6-7.

bindu. . ."[36] From the *bindu* springs the line, a continuum of infinite *bindus*. Dance is all about how the *bindu* radiates from the *nābhi,* becomes the line and returns again to the *bindu.* How it straightens out, swerves, swirls and finally goes into a spin.[37] Most of the *mudrās* (movements and postures of the hands and body) are common to both, the ritual worship as well as in dance.[38]

The reciprocity of the Indian arts has been beautifully expressed in a story from the *Viṣṇudharamottara Purāṇa.* King Vajra wanted to learn the art of image-making (sculpture) from Sage Mārkaṇḍeya, who then revealed to the king the inter-relatedness of the various branches of knowledge. In order to make one beautiful piece of sculpture, the king had to learn the arts of drawing, painting, dancing, music (vocal and instrumental), literature, language, grammar, prosody along with physical science, and the list goes on.[39] *Viṣṇudharamottara* (3.35, 5-7) points to the close relationship between painting (*citra*) and dance (*nṛtta*), which it says is a supreme art, in which there is a faithful delineation of the three worlds, through

---

36. Mātaṅga Muni, *Bṛhaddeśī,* vol. II, ed. Prem Lata Sharma and A. Beohar, IGNCA, Motilal Banarsidass, Delhi, 1994, vol. I, 2.19, pp. 6-7.

37. *Indian Dance. The Ultimate Metaphor,* ed. Shanta Serbjeet Singh, Ravi Kumar, Artemisia Ltd., Hong Kong, Bookwish (India) Pvt. Ltd., New Delhi.

    The author would like to point out that when she was learning dance, her *guru,* Sri Vikram Singh, would always tell her to take the movements from the body, and the manner, in which he expressed through his hands, *āṅgika abhinaya,* was as if he was taking the movement out from the *nābhi.*

38. See Ch. on Yantra.

39. *Viṣṇudharamottara Purāṇa,* infra, 3.35, 5-7.

    Prem Lata Sharma, *Indian Aesthetics and Musicology* (*The Art and Science of Indian Music*), ed. Urmila Sharma, Amnaya Prakashan, Bharat Nidhi, Varanasi, 2000, p. 251.

a very beautiful use of the movements of the limbs, the glances, moods and emotions. Sivaramamurti says: "This close connection is specially noteworthy because the various *sthānas* and *karaṇas* which are essential in *Nāṭya* are equally important in *citra,* wherein beauty of pose is as important as beauty of form." He also says that the different *sthānas*, *karaṇas* and the movements with gyrations forming the varied *recitakas*, *cāris* and *bhrāmaraks*, the suggestive use of the *hastas*, expressive of infinite meaning, the patting dancing feet, different from the "expressive graceful rhythmic movement and sway of limbs in *nāṭya* are all elements, as appealing in their picturesque and pleasing succession of one large never-ending series of pictures of sculpturesque effect with breath and life and movement; and indeed painting and sculpture have largely drawn on the resources of this great art for representing some of the most beautiful poses and situations. . . ."[40] The *Śilpa Prakāśa,* an Orissan text, dealing with the art of architecture, is profusely illustrated with line drawings, and reveals profound tāntric influence.[41] The *Aparājitapṛcchā,* a *śilpa* text of north India, Gujarat compiled by Bhuvandevācārya, dated about twelfth century AD, also dwells upon metaphysical manifestations and understandings of the origin and development of the universe, earth, *vāstu* and *dharma.*[42] Both the *Bṛhaddeśī* (ninth or tenth century AD), and the *Saṅgītaratnākara,* (thirteenth century AD), reveal Yogic, Tāntric and Āyurvedic influences in the understanding of the body system, its physiology and the manifestation and articulation of sound/*nāda* in *saṅgīta.* The enumeration of apparently non-musical elements in

40. C. Sivaramamurti, *Nataraja in Art Thought and Literature,* infra, p. 9.

41. *Śilpa Prakāśa,* vide Alice Boner, *Principles of Composition,* infra., p. XIV.

42. *Aparājitaprecchā — A Critical Study,* Encyclopaedic Manual on Art, *op. cit.*

the *lakṣaṇa*s of a *vaggyekāra* (composer of lyrics and music of songs), the *piṇḍotpatti prakaraṇa* in the *Saṅgītaratnākara*, along with the various stories, taken from the Purāṇas (mythology/history), performed by the dancers provide a vital link of the proof of the interrelationship between the different streams of our culture. The *Nāṭya-Śāstra* explicitly states that *citra*s (paintings) should be drawn on the walls of the *nāṭya maṇḍapa*, which may also be decorated with sculptures of animals.[43] Kramrische explains:

> The traditions of the Indian craftsman are the means and ways by which professional activity transforms knowledge of principle into practice. The knowledge of principle is imported to him through tradition. Principle is the source and origin of his calling and is known by the name of Brahma or Viśvakarmā, the sum total of creative consciousness . . . this is how the sacred texts, the Āgamas, Purāṇas and Vastūśāstras trace back the tradition of the craftsman to the fountainhead. . . .[44]

Thus, the approach of the Indian art is a holistic approach and the realization of the interrelatedness of the various arts is a result of this holistic approach. The reason is simple : all arts recreate life and its multiple experiences. The medium for creation and experience is the human body and for this reason one supplements the other. For no other reason, the best descriptions make use of borrowed similes and epithets: a painting/sculpture becomes infused with life and starts to breathe and dance; a dancer freezes to become a painting/statue; prose in its highest levels of exuberance becomes poetic, poetry becomes a song; and music becomes divine; the notes of the singer/ instrumentalist dance, while a dancer starts to sing through

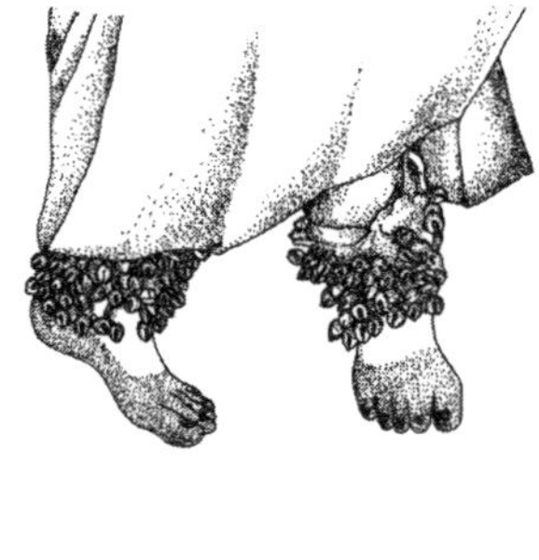

43. *Nāṭya-Śāstra*, 2.83-89, *op. cit.*, with commentaries *Madhusūdanī*, *Bālakrīḍā*, infra, pp. 188-91.
44. Stella Kramrische, *Exploring India's Sacred Art*, ed. Barbara Stroller Miller, Philadelphia, 1983, p. 59.

the body and dance becomes a lyrical expression of movements. Needless to say that the dancer's canvas is the space, his whole body is the brush and his emotions are the colours !

The basis for divine experience, *Ānanda,* is *Rasa,* and any work of art achieves perfection, if and when it succeeds in creating *rasa. Taittirīyopaniṣad* expressly states: *raso vai saḥ: rasama hyevāyam labdhvā snandi bhavati.*[45] The central point of aesthetics in the Indian tradition is *Rasa* rather than Beauty, ". . . *Rasa,* being the direct source or essence of *Ānanda,* is the ultimate goal of all artistic creation. Needless to add, that it is also the essence of Beauty."[46] *Nāṭya-Śāstra,* the earliest extant book on dramaturgy, states that Brahmā took *Rasa* from *Atharvaveda.*[47] The analogy used by Bharata for the enjoyment of art is from the mundane world, relish or taste,[48] yet in art the experience becomes *alaukika,* i.e., out of the world experience, because there is no *duḥkha* or sorrow in this experience. According to Bhaṭṭanāyaka, in the artistic experience and expression of beauty, the *rajas* and *tamas bhāvas* are overpowered in the heart of the *sahṛdaya* (connoisseur) by the *sattva bhāvas. Sattva-guṇa* is *prakāśātmaka* (full of light), and *ānandātamaka* (full of joy). Thus, the total experience results in bringing tranquillity to the mind.[49] According to Bhaṭṭanāyaka the flow of *rasa* is

45. *Taittirīyopaniṣad,* 2.7.1.

46. Prem Lata Sharma, *Indian Aesthetics and Musicology (The Art and Science of Indian Music),* infra., p. 99.

47. *Nāṭya-Śāstra,* 1.16-17, *op. cit.,* with commentaries *Madhusūdanī, Bālakrīḍā,* p. 56.

48. *Ibid.,* 6.2, also see commentary, pp. 592-94. Also see Prem Lata Sharma, *Indian Aesthetics and Musicology (The Art and Science of Indian Music), op. cit.,* p. 99-100.

49. *Saṅgīta Darśana Paricarcā Smārikā,* ed. N. Rajam, BHU, Varanasi, 1986, in which is published, "Viniyoga, Kalāoṅ kā Saundaryānubhūti me," (Hindi), Article by Brajmohan Chaturvedi, p. 51.

more easy and enjoyable, *sarasa,* in the practice of arts as compared to the other yogic *kriyās* (practises). Ācārya Abhinavagupta also states that the aesthetic experience is similar to spiritual experience. The arts become a medium for raising the level of *sattva* in the artist/connossieur, and thus the cause for the experience of *Ānanda*. He calls this aesthetic experience *svātmaparāmarśa,* a state where there is total unification of the mind with the soul, when this happens the person forgets his purpose, objective and even himself.[50] This is the stage *par excellence,* when the lover becomes the beloved and, the beloved the lover ! Kr̥ṣṇa becoming Rādhā and Rādhā becoming Kr̥ṣṇa has been the subject of various paintings (see *Pls.* 11, 12, 13), as well as many songs, *ṭhumarīs*, and *rasiyāsa,* which over the years have enriched the repertoire of *Kathaka.*[51] This state is

50. *Saṅgīta Darśana Paricarcā Smārikā,* ed. N. Rajam, BHU, Varanasi, 1986, p. 51.

51. Today, however, with the fast changing cultural scenario, largely as a result of the impact of globalization, in the mask of modernity much of our cultural wisdom/heritage transmitted over the years is being lost. Dance no longer remains a *sādhanā*. The commercial aspect has become stronger, as a result the itinerary and the repertoire of *Kathaka* has changed to include challenging themes which have no bearing on the religio-social aspect. Also compare Prem Lata Sharma, *Indian Aesthetics and Musicology* (*The Art and Science of Indian Music*), infra., pp. 84-85, wherein she voices similar thought: "The co-mingling of the divine and the mundane necessarily contained a few anomalies hitherto unnoticed or connived at, which came to surface forcibly with the change in the general social outlook during the last two centuries. They have given rise to a steadily growing widespread scepticism, bordering on hostility towards this literature. A serious misunderstanding of the content, nature and scope of the aforesaid composite character of this literature arose out of an abrupt change in social outlook and values as a result of the impact of the cataclysm of scientific discoveries. It led notable thinkers to throw up this literature of millenniums in utter despair as more or less meaningless and invalid."

referred to as *hāva* (external indications of love), which is occasioned by the union of the hero and the heroine.[52] The loosing or melting of oneself and forgetting one's existence for that time best takes place in *Nāṭya*. *Nṛtta* as a part of *Nāṭya* thus becomes efficacious as a medium for apprehending the all-pervading unity in the diversity of names and forms (*nāma* and *rūpa*), just as a dancer enacts

---

52. *Hāva* may be of thirteen kinds :
    (a) *Līlā-hāva* — when the lovers imitate each other in manners and dress, etc.
    (b) *Vilāsa-hāva* — when the eyes of the heroine shine with delight.
    (c) *Lalita-hāva* — when charm is generated through speech, laughter, voluptuous grace.
    (d) *Vichchiti-hāva* — when the personal charm supersedes external decorations, ornaments.
    (e) *Vibhrama-hāva* — when the sight of the lover flusters the beloved into making wrong movements.
    (f) *Kilakiñchitā-hāva* — when there is a mixed expression of various emotion — a kind of hysterical delight.
    (g) *Mottāyita-hāva* — are mute involuntary expressions of affection — *sāttvika bhāva*.
    (h) *Bibboka-hāva* — when the heroine pretends to be indifferent to the arrival of her lover and makes a false show of anger.
    (i) *Helā-hāva* — when the heroine under the influence of love forgets her modesty.
    (j) *Bodha-hāva* or *Bodhaka-hāva* — when the hero expresses his feelings through signs or riddles.
    (k) *Kuttamita-hāva* — when simulated quarrels in the midst of love sport add to the joy of love.
    (l) *Mada-hāva* — is the expression of arrogance arising from love.
    (m) *Vikṛtā-hāva* — when *nāyaka* or *nāyikā* are not able to speak due to bashfulness.

    For more details see M.S. Randhawa, *Kangra Paintings on Love*, National Museum, New Delhi, 1962, pp. 52-62.

different roles with corresponding different emotions without there being any reality of those roles and emotions in her own self. This is the secret concept of Guhya.[53] *Nāṭya* as we know is one of the most ancient forms of the language of worship. The symbolism used in *nāṭya*, the gestures, postures, which form part of the *nṛtta* code are also part of the tāntric ritual. Ācārya Abhinavagupta, the writer of the *Abhinavabhāratī* (commentary on *Nāṭya-Śāstra*), refers to the tāntric concept of Śiva and Śakti, well associated with tāntric *sādhanā*, in this commentary.[54] As earlier said, in

---

53. Prem Lata Sharma, *Indian Aesthetics and Musicology*, infra, pp. 99-101, wherein she explains, "The cause and effect relationship inherent in different situations of life, when depicted through drama tends to free the audience from the *Rāga-Dveṣa* (attraction and repulsion) and enables them to relish the *bhāva* in its universalized साधारणीकृत state without any particularities or limitations of space, time or individual entity (देश, काल, पात्र). Hence, artistic enjoyment is *alaukika* i.e. unlike the common experiences of life. It cannot be equated with memory, imagination or direct experience. That experience brings about the cessation of all mental activity (संविद्विश्रान्ति) for the duration of its own existence. It brings about temporary liberation of the mind from bondages of "I-ness" and makes possible the experience of basic mental states (स्थायि भाव) in their individualized form. The mind becomes free from all "particular" or binding or limiting factors of a given situation which accompany it in actual life. Thus, there is a perfect blending of *tāṭasthya* (neutrality) and *tādātmya* (identification) i.e., the audience completely identifies with the given situation and is at the same time detached or neutral because the situation does not affect their actual personal life in any way. . . That is why even painful situations become enjoyable in drama." Also see Kumbhā Rāṇā, *Saṅgītarāja*, ed. Prem Lata Sharma, Hindu Vishvavidyalaya Sanskrit Pub. Board, BHU, Varanasi, 1963, p. 94.

54. Abhinavagupta, *Abhinavabhāratī*, 2, vide *Nāṭya-Śāstra* with commentaries *Madhusūdanī Bālakrīḍā*, infra., p. 4. Refers to the 36 *tattva*s, which are actually the manifestation of the *Śivatattva* in the universe.

nāṭya are embodied all the sciences, epics and arts. The association of *nṛtta* (dance) with worship and ritual is age old. The *Nāṭya-maṇḍapa* was specially created and devoted to the exposition of Bharata's *Nāṭya-Śāstra,* in the presence of Naṭarāja, the Lord of dance, himself, who is described as *Sarvatūryaninādī.*[55] *Nāṭya-Śāstra* clearly refers to the ritual of the worship of *raṅga* (stage) and the *jarajara* (the staff of Viṣṇu) as akin to the performance of *yajña,* accompanied with the chanting of *mantra*s, for the shower of blessings on the actors, dancers and the instruments.[56]

Dance is thus a visual representation of the manifestation of *Nāda.* It is imaging sound. It is the highest form of yogic activity and reveals the impact of Tantra in its various concepts of *mudrā, āsana, prāṇāyama,* etc. Whether Yoga, Tantra or *Nṛtta,* the effort is to go within one's self in order to experience the oneness, *Ānanda* or Bliss. For this reason the great exponents of dance, apart from the Trinity Brahmā-Viṣṇu-Śiva, also include Indra, Ādityas, Rudras, Vāsus and many other celestials like Gandharvas, Haṁsa, the highest of the Vidyādharas, Hāhā, Hūhū, Bṛhaspati, Tumburu, Viśvāvasu and Apsarās, like Menakā, Sahjanyā, Parṇinī, Puñjikasthala, Ghṛtācī, Urvaśī and many others.[57]

The art form *Kathaka,* in its own unique and subtle style/ way of expression, incorporates within itself the knowledge and skill of these various *śāstra*s. The very first stance in which the dancer stands in *samapāda samabhaṅga* holding a *samadaṁśa- mudrā* (described as *Hamsāsya hasta* in the *Abhinaya Darpaṇa*). in the hands, palms facing down, arms bent from the elbow a little lower than the chest, reveals a

55. C. Sivaramamurti, *Nataraja in Art Thought and Literature* infra., p. 2, wherein he gives the reference of *Liṅga Purāṇa,* 1, 65, 82, 84.

56. *Nāṭya-Śāstra,* infra. 3.83-89, p. 159 and 2.1 p. 217-18.

57. C. Sivaramamurti, *Nataraja in Art Thought and Literature,* infra p. 3.

yogic posture[58] (see *Pl.* 14, 15 and *figs.* 2 & 3). The controlled rhythmic breathing (*prāṇāyāma*) to the sound of accompanying music, the eyes half closed, the body moving/swaying gently, from one side to the other in the manner of a flame, reveals a clear impact of Tantra. This entire *prakriyā* (movement/process) is termed as *śulu*.[59] The body is conceived like a *diyā* (earthen lamp) and through *prāṇāyāma*, the fire is kindled and lighted, the force of which is expressed in the soft swaying of the body. It is after this that the body goes into movement as an expression of the *nāda* and creates images and pictures, *yantra*s (lines, dots, circles, triangles) not only in space but also on the ground below, along with the *paḍhanta* (recitation) of apparently meaningless syllables, also referred to as *pāṭhya*, which covers syllabic sounds accompanied by *kāku svara* and *chanda* or may we call them *mantra*s ?

On the more material or gross level, this may be taken to correspond to the control of the subtle body through *prāṇāyāma* and the control of the physical body through *Haṭha Yoga* (use of postures, (*āsana*s), etc.). *Prāṇāyāma* or controlled breathing not only sets a specific vibration/rhythm but it also helps in the process of concentration, the two being inter-dependent. Nik Douglas says,

---

58. *Samapāda* : when both the feet are naturally placed flat on the ground with a distance of eight-ten *aṅgula*s. It gives firmness and balance to the body and mind. This is the *sthānaka* of Brahmā. *Samabhaṅga* : when the torso is straight without any bends or inflexions or deflexions. It gives firmness and balance to the body and mind. *Samadaṁśa* : when the tip of the forefinger and the thumb touch each other, with the other fingers opening out as in breaking flowers or pulling out a thorn. It is also known as the *cina-mudrā*, i.e., the *mudrā* used in meditation. Also see Ch. on Tantra.

59. *Śulū* : *Deśinṛttam*, See Bharata Koṣa, Ramkrishna Kavi, Munshiram Manoharlal, 1961, p. 737.

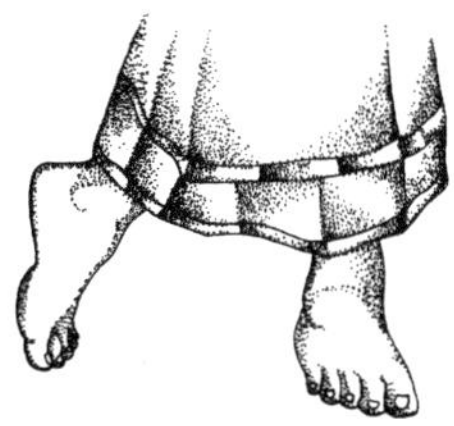

Breath movement (*prāṇāyāma*) is closely related to inner sound (*śabda*); the subtle body to *mantra, yantra* and to *āsana* (body posture). A body has *yantra* (form) by the nature of its posture (*āsana*). It has *mantra* by the nature of its breathing *prāṇāyāma*.[60]

The navel, variously termed as the *ghanībhūta bindu*, the *brahmagranthī* or the *bindu*, is equally important in dance as it is in *Tantra-Śāstra*. Though the *Nāṭya-Śāstra* does not explicitly deal with *nābhi,* but it recognizes the Āyurvedic and Yogic conception of the navel as the centre of the body and thus body movements as well as the universe. It is also the centre of energy. *Saṅgītaratnākara* describes the body in detail and calls it *brahmagranthī* (the knot of *brahman*). The symbolical aspect of the navel which in *Tantra-Śāstra* is described as a lotus with ten petals, has been derived from the Viṣṇu myth — Viṣṇu as *padmanābha*. The *yogin* makes an effort with concentration to arrive at the central point of the navel from where he may be able to catch a direct path connected with higher planes of consciousness, while to a common man of phenomenal vision, the navel as the centre of activity pulls him down to the world of work and activity.[61] The *Saṅgītaratnākara* also states that the *maṇipūra*

60. Nik Douglas, *Tantra Yoga*, Munshiram Manoharlal, New Delhi, 1991, p. 65.

61. *Kalātattvakośa*, vol. II, IGNCA, New Delhi, 1992, pp. 43-44. It also states that while describing the 14 locations for the movements of the hands (*karakṣetra*) in dance, S.R. VII, 546-47ab — describes the movement of the hands held at the level of or touching the navel. The central position of the navel in dance has to do with the balance of the human body (*sana*) — with the navel as the centre and the spinal cord as the vertical median, various positions are evolved in dance.

Also the author's *guru* told her to bring out the movements from the body, but the *āṅgika* used by him to express was as if catching something about the navel area and bringing it out.

cakra, also called the *nābhi padma*, is located around the region of the root of the navel, and so is also referred to as the *navel cycle*. The *Gautamīya Tantra* states that owing to the presence of the fiery *tejas* (brilliance), this centre is lustrous as a gem (*maṇi*) and so is called *maṇipūra*.[62]

We could thus safely conclude that dance as one of the constituents of *saṅgīta*, also constitutes as a part of *Nāṭya*, the *pañcama Veda*, and is thus repudiated by Śruti. Tantra (Āgama) as an off-shoot of Nigama is also an established fact. The impact of Tantra at a particular period of time cannot be ruled out. The *āsanas*, *mudrās*, *maṇḍalas*, *prāṇāyāma*, *dhyānas*, *nāyaka-nāyikā-bheda* bear a clear mark of the tāntric tradition. In fact, the *rāga dhyāna*s exhibit a close and distinct impact of the theory of the *nāyaka-nāyikā-bheda*. The seed syllables of notes or *pātākṣara*s, perhaps, reflect the influence of Tantra on the already existing tradition of Vedic *saṅgīta*. Every seed syllable (*bījākṣara*) has a presiding deity in the tāntric *śāstra* while the hymns in the Vedic tradition, the *sūkta*s, also have a presiding deity, along with a *seer* and a *chanda* (metre); *Nāda* is not just sound, it is worshipped as *parā-vāc*, the energy of *Brahman*, or as *Nāda-Brahman*. It is the cause of the manifest universe. The creative power of this absolute *Brahman* is referred to as *kuṇḍalinī* or the Śakti of Śiva in *Tantra Yoga*. It lies coiled like a serpent, and only through the process of intense meditation it uncoils, rushing up to the *brahmarandhra* (lit. the doorway to the Absolute), the mystic cerebral aperture, resulting in an experience of Absolute Bliss. The Indian arts of music and dance are an extension of the Vedic, Tāntric and Yogic practices and thus powerful and potent instruments for the religious, social and spiritual upliftment of man and mankind.

62. Vide *Saṅgītaratnākara*, vol. I, 1-2.124-25, tr. R.K. Shringey & Prem Lata Sharma, infra., p. 89.

2

Mantra

THE importance of *mantras* on the Indian social-cultural religious scene is unquestioned. From the womb of the mother to the funeral pyre, the ritualistic life of the Indian people reveals a preponderance of the use of *mantras* in the form of chanting of *mantras* or singing of hymns. *Nāṭya-Śāstra* by Bharat Muni clearly states that there is nothing greater in the whole universe than *vāc* or *vāṇī*, which is also the cause of the universe.[1] In a culture which has given

1. Bharata Muni, *Nāṭya-Śāstra*, 14.3, vol. II, p. 1159, with commentary *Abhinavabhāratī* by Abhinavaguptācārya along with commentaries *Madhusūdanī* and *Bālakrīḍā*, Banaras Hindu University, 1975. Also see Muni Mātaṅga, *Bṛhaddeśī*, 1.1.42, pp. 4-5, Kalāmūlaśāstra Series (8) ed. Kapila Vatsyayan, IGNCA, Motilal Banarsidass, Delhi, 1992, wherein it is said "*Dhvani* is the ultimate origin (*yoni*, lit. womb); *dhvani* is the cause of everything. The whole world of immobile and mobile (beings) is, encompassed by *dhvani* (12). Also see Śāraṅgadeva, *Saṅgītaratnākara*, 1.2.1-2, vol. I, p. 20, Sanskrit Text and English Translation with Comments and Notes by R.K. Shringy and Prem Lata Sharma, Munshiram Manoharlal, wherein it is stated. "*Nāda*, as already stated, is primordial sound considered by some of the schools of Indian Philosophy, specially *Yoga* and *Tantra*, to be the primary cause of the phenomenal world. Of the five basic elements, earth, water, fire, air and ether, perceived correspondingly by the sense of smell, taste, vision, touch and hearing, ether is the most pervasive and the cause of the rest. Sound is considered to be the manifestation of *Nāda*, which is described as *Nāda-Brahman* and is thus equated with the absolute of the Upaniṣads"; also see p. 23, where

→

so much importance to *vāc* as being of divine origin, *mantras* may be defined as phonic forms of a transcendent reality. According to Wheelock, they are "sonic manifestations of basic cosmic powers : they are the cosmic elements in essential form."[2] The importance of sound was realized by our ancient seers and they bequeathed a legacy of *Nāda-Brahman* (as used in the *Saṅgīta-Śāstra*) or the *Śabda-Brahman* (as used in the *Vyākaraṇa-Śāstra*) or the *sphoṭa-vāda* (as used in the *Tantra-Śāstra*, which like the Veda is also from Śruti). *Nāda* is one of the *guṇas* (attributes) of *Ākāśa* and may manifest as *āhata nāda* or *anāhata nāda*. The *anāhata nāda* vibrates as *oṁkāra* in the universe.[3] This *anāhata nāda* then takes a form and along with the form it also takes space. Both kinds of *nāda* have their origin in the human body.[4] The Upaniṣads speak of the voice as *daivī-vīṇā*, and the man-made lute as the *mānuśī-vīṇā*.[5] *Nāṭya-Śāstra* speaks of the voice as *śārīrī-vīṇā* (the body lute) and the instrument

---

→ in it is stated, "*Nāda* is the basis, not only for music and dance, though especially related to it, but of the entire business of life. Since it constitutes the very substance of speech. . .". Also see Kumbhā Mahārāṇā, *Saṅgitarāja*, Gītaratnakośa, vol. I, vs. 20-23, p. 73, ed. Prem Lata Sharma, Hindu Vishvavidyalaya, Sanskrit Pub. Board, 1963, where *nāda* is described as the product of two *śaktis*, *prāṇa* and *agni* and as the source of *ānanda* it is composed of seeds (*bīja*) of Ādya Śakti.

2. Andre Padoux, *Mantras — What are they* ? Other details missing.
3. Śāraṅgadeva, *Saṅgītaratnākara*, 1.2.126, vol. I, p. 90, *op. cit.* The translation reads, "In the heart is located the psycho-physical centre called the cycle of the unmanifest (*anāhata cakra*, with twelve petals which is considered to be the place of worshipping Lord Śiva in the form of *oṁ*. (126-27b)."
4. Śāraṅgadeva, *Saṅgītaratnākara*, 1.2.3, vol. I, p. 23, *ibid.*
5. Prem Lata Sharma, "Relationship Between Voice and Instruments in the Indian Tradition," Article published, other details missing.

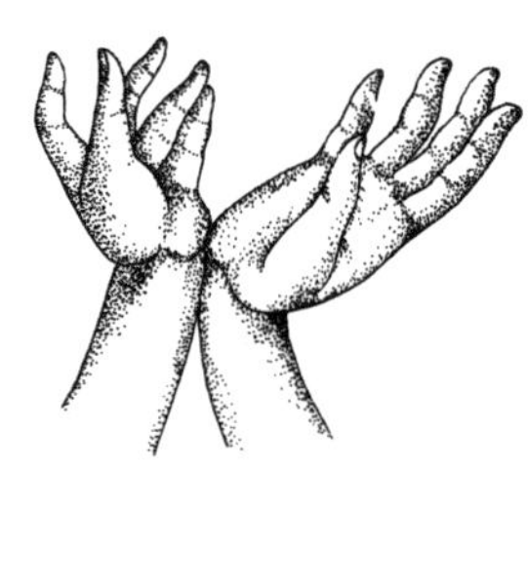

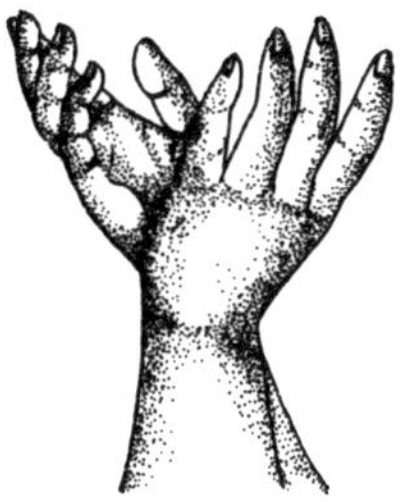

lute as the *dāravī-vīṇā* (wooden lute).[6] *Nāṭya-Śāstra* also states sound to be two-fold : *svaravāna* (tonal) and *abhidhānavāna* (having a meaning). It says that *svaras* (tones) are first born on the bodily *vīṇā*, and then they are transmitted to the wooden *vīṇā* (which includes the aerophones) then they go to the drums and then to the cymbals.[7] The *Abhinaya Darpaṇa* also makes a reference to the same thought, but with a difference, to quote Sivaramamurti, ". . . the sequence in dance is given in a verse, the song to be sustained in the throat, meaning rendered by the hands, the moods (*bhāva*) delivered by the glances, and the rhythm (*tāla*) marked by the feet."[8] He also states that Sarasvatī, the goddess of learning, music and dance, with a *vīṇā* in her hand is almost the counterpart of Vīṇādhara Śiva.[9] Every sound apart from having a *spandana* (vibration), of a certain intensity, density, a specific quality of space, has another quality, it is the quality of light as pointed out by Daṇḍī : "The entirety of the three worlds would have been dark blind, if the light of sound does not shine brightly in the world of existence."[10] As one of the *guṇas* of *ākāśa*, *nāda* is both *sūkṣma* (subtle) and *vyāpaka*

---

6. *Ibid.*, *Nātya-Śāstra*, XXVIII.12-15, Sharma also elaborates that in the Indian tradition the human body has been accepted to be a *vīṇā* and not as a flute as in the Sūfī tradition.
7. *Ibid.*, *Nātya-Śāstra*, XXXIV.28-31, vide Prem Lata Sharma article, "Relationship Between voice and Instruments in the Indian Tradition."
8. C. Sivaramamurti, *Naṭarāja In Art Thought And Literature*, Publication Division, Ministry of Information and Broadcasting, Govt. of India, 1974, p. 14.
9. *Ibid.*
10. H.N. Chakravarty, Mantra and the Significance of Repetitive Sounds, Paper read in the National Seminar on "Dhvani," *Jñāna Pravāha*, Centre for Cultural Studies, Varanasi, March 11-14th, 1999.

(widespread).[11]

Both the *Bṛhaddeśī* (1.20)[12] and the *Saṅgītaratnākara* (1.3.6),[13] explain *Nāda* as the interaction or combination of *na* with *da*. *Na* represents the vital force or *prāṇa* (air) and *da* represents fire. Kallinath, the commentator of the *Saṅgītaratnākara*, explains that *na* and *da* should not be taken as letters or words representing ordinary speech or language, but should be understood as the *bījākṣaras* of *Mantra-Śāstra*. Every *bījākṣara* according to the *Tantra-Śāstra* has a presiding deity, and in this reference the letters *na* and *da* refer to *prāṇa* and *agni*, i.e., the vital force and fire.[14] According to Padoux,

> . . . *mantras* in some of their forms the *bījas* mostly answer the deeply ingrained urge to emit sounds that are both arbitrary (i.e., not part of language or linguistic use) and not innocent (i.e., having a meaning or evoking something).[15]

To quote R.A. Paul :

> These syllables are without discursive meaning, but they must be so since they are generative elements, not surface structures: a seed does not display the likeness of a stalk of wheat, not does a drop of semen resemble a man.[16]

Saṅgītaratnākara (1.3.1) refers to the worship of *Nāda-Brahman* as the incomparable bliss which is immanent in all creatures, as *caitanya* (intelligence), and is found manifest in all creatures

---

11. Prem Lata Sharma, *Indian Aesthetics and Musicology* (*The Art and Science of Indian Music*), vol. I, ed. U. Sharma, Amnāya-Prakāśana, Bharata-Nidhi, Varanasi, 2000.
12. Mataṅga Muni, *Bṛhaddeśī*, vol. I. 1.20, p. 9, infra.
13. Śāraṅgadeva, *Saṅgītaratnākara*, vol. I, 1.3.6, p. 113, *op. cit.*
14. *Ibid.*
15. Andre Padoux, *Mantras — What Are they* ? Other details missing.
16. *Ibid.*, in which there is a reference to the Tibetan Symbolic work : *Psychoanalytic Explorations*, Chicago, 1982, p. 30.

as well as in the phenomenon of the universe. Kallinath also equates *Nāda* with the *parāvāka śakti* of *Brahman* and by worshipping the *śakti* of *Brahman*, one can attain *Brahman* itself.[17] The entire creation arises and dissolves into the *Brahman* which is the ultimate Reality and which expresses as *Ānanda* or Bliss. Mataṅga Muni in the *Bṛhaddeśī* (2.19), states :

> Brahmā is known to be in the form of *Nāda* (*nāda rūpa*), Janārdana (Viṣṇu) is of the form of *nāḍa*, *parā śakti*, is of the form of *nāda* (and) Maheśvara is of the form of *nāda*.[18]

Saṅgītaratnākara (1.3.2), extols the worship of *Nāda*. It says that the *svarūpa* (form) of Brahmā, Viṣṇu and Maheśa is *nādātmaka* and their worship is best achieved by the worship of *nāda*.[19]

> The gods, Brahmā, Viṣṇu and Śiva in the *paurāṇika* mythology represent the three aspects of the manifestation of *Brahman* into the phenomenon of the universe, viz., creation, preservation and destruction; the three being part and parcel of a single movement called Śakti or the energy of the creative power of *Brahman*. This energy is called *Nāda* or *Śabda*, i.e., the word or the *parā vāk* as "K" puts it. In the first stage of manifestation the energy involved in *Brahman* evolves into undifferentiated consciousness which is called *Nāda-Brahman* in our text and accordingly the three gods named above are the three aspects in which the energy separates in the manifestations. *Nāda-Brahman* is also known as *Śabda-Brahman*.[20]

---

17. Śāraṅgadeva, *Saṅgītaratnākara*, vol. I, 1.3.1, pp. 101-10, infra.
18. Mataṅga Muni, *Bṛhaddeśī*, vol. I, 2.19, p. 7, *op.cit.*
19. Śāraṅgadeva, *Saṅgītaratnākara*, vol. I, 1.3.2, p. 109, infra. "As intelligence or bliss, *Nāda-Brahman* is immanent in all the beings. This immanence indicates the state of non-differentiation which is manifest in the differentiated consciousness of the universe in the relationship of the seer and the seen, the subject and the object." Kallināth also points out that *nāda* is the source of *śrutis*, letters and words, etc., on which is based the conduct of worldly affairs.
20. Śāraṅgadeva, *Saṅgītaratnākara*, 1.3.2, p. 110, *ibid.*, see notes.

In a vivid description of the *Ānandatāṇḍava* of Śiva, the *Naṭeśāṣṭaka* states :

> I seek the protection of the Lord of Chitsabhā, who calls up the entire concourse of living beings in the three worlds by the tinkling sound of the anklets on his left foot, slightly raised, who is praised by the lotus-eyed Viṣṇu and others, and who accomplishes the five essential acts, *pañcakṛtya*, creation, preservation, destruction, withdrawal of illusion and the blessing of liberation.[21]

Bṛhaddeśī, (1.11.18), clearly states:

> There is no *gīta* (song, music) without *nāda,* there are no *svara*s (musical notes) without *nāda,* there is no *nṛtta* (dance) without *nāda,* hence the world is of the essence of *nāda.*[22]

Saṅgītaratnākara (1.1.21) states that *saṅgīta* is constituted by *gītam* (vocal melody), *vādyam* (playing on instruments) and *nṛttam* (dancing).[23] *Saṅgītaratnākara* (1.1.24), further states that dancing is guided by instrumental music, which in its own turn follows the vocal music.[24] *Saṅgītaratnākara* (1.3.3-4), refers to the process of manifestation of sound in the human body. It states that the desire for self-expression is the motive power which initiates the process into action, ". . . desire for self-expression is discerned to be the cause of speech and therefore of singing i.e. music and even dance as it is included in the concept of *saṅgīta.*"[25] *Nṛttaratnāvalī* (1.4) clearly states that Śiva, the formless, assumes different forms like Sadāśiva as he delights in his own cosmic dance. Without the form He cannot dance. The appeal of dance is

21. Vide C. Sivaramamurti, *Naṭarāja In Art Thought And Literature,* p. 126, *op.cit.*
22. Mataṅga Muni, *Bṛhaddeśī,* 1.11.18, p. 7, infra.
23. Śāraṅgadeva, *Saṅgītaratnākara,* 1.1.21, p. 10, *op.cit.,* It further states *saṅgīta* to be two-fold : *mārgī* and *deśī.*
24. Śāraṅgadeva, *Saṅgītaratnākara,* p. 11, 1.1.24, *ibid.*
25. *Ibid.,* 1.3.3-4, p. 111, also see commentary.

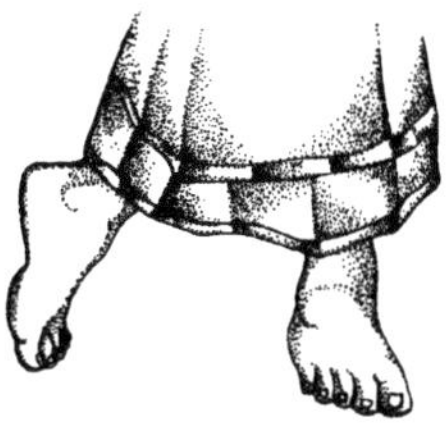

so great that even Śiva desires and chooses to assume a form to enjoy his own cosmic dance.[26] *Nṛttratnāvalī* (1.10) also states that dance brings in movement all the essential charm in the five elements : earth, water, fire, air and sky, i.e., reflection in gems, waves and ripple in water, flames in fire, movement in wind and the play in lightening[27] Sivaramamurti aptly says that the movements in dance bring together the charm of the five elements which explains the glory of Śiva himself, both as *aṣṭamūrti*s and as composed of the five elements.[28]

Dance thus as one of the constituents of *saṅgīta*, manifests through *nāda* very explicit and aesthetic movements in time and space. To put the same thought a little differently, it could be said that the movements of the dancer in time and space are a result of the expression of the awakening of the whole process of *nāda*, which in classical dance works on two levels : one, the *anāhata nāda*, which is present in the dancer himself, is aroused from the *mūlādhāra* when the dancer desires to express his *bhāva*s or feelings, and the other is in the nature of accompaniments for dance, i.e., the musicians (singers, instrumentalists), where the manifestation comes out at the level of *vaikharī*, the unifying principle being *dhvani*. In the *Nāṭya-Śāstra* (14.2), Bharata explicitly says that *vāṇī* is the *tana* or *śarīra* (body) of any *nāṭya* performance. All the three *abhinaya*s are in fact expressions of the *vāc*.[29]

---

26. Vide C. Sivaramamurti, *Naṭarāja In Art Thought And Literature*, infra, p. 11.
27. *Ibid.*, p. 12.
28. *Ibid.*, wherein he says, "Śiva is a great dancer. He assumes forms only for enjoying his dance, and there are forms appropriate for dance, and the five elements in their respective movements only suggest the rhythmic movements in dance. . . ."
29. Bharata Muni, *Nāṭya-Śāstra*, 14.2, p. 1149, *op. cit.*, *vācika abhinaya* has been left out because it is self-explanatory.

Saṅgītaratnākara (7.2-4), states that *nartana* is three-fold; *nāṭya, nṛtta* and *nṛtya.*[30] *Saṅgītaratnākara* (7.16-19), states that *nāṭya* primarily means *rasa* (sentiment), through implication, dancing which makes *rasa* manifest and consists of the four types of *abhinaya* (gestures) is said to be *nāṭya* by the learned.[31] Thus, the interrelatedness, interdependence of *gīta, vādya* and *nṛtta. Saṅgītaratanākara* (1.2.1), meaningfully states : *nāda* is the very essence of vocal music. Instrumental music is enjoyable as it manifests *nāda. Nṛtta* (dance) follows both (i.e., vocal and instrumental music); therefore all the three depend upon *nāda.*[32]

We could thus safely deduce that dance as an expression of *form-language,* is not intrinsically different from verbal symbolism, except that it works through a different medium. But while the symbolism of word images is readily understood and accepted, as is immediately visible in the works of the great poet-dramatist, Kālīdasa or later in the *Gīta Govinda* of Jayadeva, which abound in creating *vāc* images infused with great pictorial quality, the symbol value of images/forms created in the arts of painting, sculpture and dancing is often missed immediately. Yet, as we have seen, both *word* and *form* originate from the same source. To quote Boner,

> They are both emanations of the supreme Life force and both stand as symbols for transcendent Reality. But since they are two different channels through which the spirit works they act upon different faculties in man. This is the reason why there can never be absolute equation between

30. Śāraṅgadeva, *Saṅgītaratnākara,* vol. IV, 7.2-4, p. 3, The Adyar Library and Research Centre, Madras, 1953.
31. *Ibid.,* 7.16-19, pp. 7-8, also see *Saṅgītaratnākara,* tr. Kunjunni Raja and Radha Bernier, The Adyar Library and Reseach Centre, Madras, 1976, pp. 2-3.
32. Śāraṅgadeva, *Saṅgītaratnākara,* 1.2.1-2, ed. R.K. Shringey and Prem Lata Sharma, *op. cit.,* pp. 21-22.

> the expressions of the one and of the other. . . . A concept expressed in words and sounds cannot be transferred into signs and figures without taking on entirely new connotations. Auditive expression works in time while visual expression works in space.[33]

It would be worthwhile to make a reference to Sivaramamurti, who explicitly says that dance thus as *vyañjanā* or suggestion becomes superior to *abhidhā* or utterance. To quote,

> The different *sthānas* and *karaṇas* comprising the infinite poses and the movements with gyrations forming the varied *recitas*, *cāris* and *bhramarakas*, the suggestive use of *hastas* including the numerous *asaṁyukta* and *saṁyukta* ones, each one of the former variety expressive of infinite meaning, and richer still in its connotation when combined in different modes to form the *hastas* of the latter variety, the special movement of the eye, neck and hip, constituting the lovely notes of the pat of the feet, making up the pure and orderly *nṛtta*. . . are all elements, as appealing in their picturesque and pleasing succession of one large never-ending series of pictures of sculpturesque effect with breath and life and movement.[34]

The power inherent in *Nāda* or *saṅgīta* has been the subject of laudation in many Purāṇas and other ancient literature. One of the Purāṇas very clearly states that *dhyāna* is more than *pūjā*, *japa* is more than *dhyāna*, *gāna* is more than *japa* and there is nothing more than *gāna*,[35] *Śrīmada Bhāgavata* (10.21) (ch. on *Veṇu Gīta*) and the *Saṅgītaratnākara*

---

33. Alice Boner, *Principles of Composition in Hindu Sculpture: Cave Temple Period*, p. 13, Leiden, E.J. Brill, Netherlands, 1962.
34. C. Sivaramamurti, *Naṭarāja In Art Thought And Literature*, *op.cit.*, p. 11.
35. C. Sivaramamurti, *Naṭarāja In Art Thought And Literature*, *op.cit.*, pp. 132, 137, 128.

(6.768.1097, 1125),[36] refer to the magical effect of the sound produced on the *veṇu* (flute) of Śrī Kṛṣṇa : In the river the lotus begins to sprout, intoxicated peacocks begin to dance, cows and trees begin to shed tears, etc., etc., and yet the entire forest becomes *spandanahīna*. Similarly, the *tāṇḍava* dance performed by Śiva, creates thunderous sound comparable to the deafening sound of the cavalry of the Kākatīya army, the uninterrupted thuds of the hoofs of horses, or even the sportive light footsteps, with only the forepart of the foot touching the ground which gladdens his consort Pārvatī and the other celestials. The strong resounding sound bends the earth, terrifies the quarters and frightens the Lord of the celestials to shriek and still he performs/dances the *nādānta*. Devī, the eternal witness of Śiva's dance and Herself a great dancer, performs in the mode of *lāsya*. The resounding sound which is produced through her dance is *hṛīṁkāra*, her favourite monosyllabic sound, *hṛīṁkārasthāna-nartakī*.[37]

All the gods and goddesses in the Hindu pantheon are associated with at least one musical instrument : the *ḍamaru* of Śiva, the *nupuras* of Viṣṇu, the flute of Kṛṣṇa, the *mṛdaṅga* of Gaṇapati, the *vīṇā* of Sarasvatī. The ruling deity of the *nupuras* (bells) are the *nakṣatras*.[38] The three principle deities delight in dance.

> The wonderful sweet ocular appeal of dance is so inviting that Śiva, Kṛṣṇa and Brahmā practise dance with their respective consorts. . . .
>
> — *Nṛttaratnāvalī* (1.5)[39]

36. *Śrīmad Bhāgawat*, 10-21, along with commentary in Hindi by Golokavali Lala Shaligramji Vaishya, Khemraj Srikrsnadasa, Bombay also see Prem Lata Sharma, the *Alchemy of Love and Wisdom, op. cit.*, p. 110.
37. C. Sivaramamurti, *Naṭarāja In Art Thought And Literature*, infra, p. 128.
38. *Abhinaya Darpaṇa*, 30, tr. P. Dadicha, p. 10, Bindu Prakashan, Ujjain, 1988. .

Thus, *vāc* may be *nirukta* (defined) or *anirukta* (undefined); it manifests in all living and non-living beings/things, e.g., instruments. *Mantra*s as manifestations of *vāc/nāda*, reveal two powers : the *vācaka* and the *vācya*. They are inseparably united to each other and are termed *vimarśa* and *prakāśa* in the Śaiva doctrine.[40] Elucidating the above idea, the ancient thinkers saw the world thus :

> In the *vācaka* level they view the world as composed of three components. They are known as *parā, sūkṣma* and *sthūla,* extremely subtle, subtle and gross, designated as *varṇa, mātrā* and *pada*. This is the manifestation of the *vācaka* aspect, while in the manifestation of the *vācya* aspect they shine as highly subtle. Then it is known as *kalā*. The number of *kalā*s is five which assumes the form of *tattva*s. These *tattva*s according to the Śaiva view are 36. In each of the *tattva*s there are *bhuvanas;* worlds made of *tattva*s and *tattva*s in their turn are made of subtle *kalā*s.[41]

As *tattva*s are made of *kalā*s, so they gain their existence from *varṇa*s. For example, the fifty syllables from "अ" to "क्ष" are associated with each *tattva*s and they are essentially in the nature of *varṇa*s. These *varṇa*s, when they are agitated, give rise to *mantra*s. The *Tantra-Śāstra* clearly states that while the *mantra*s are composed of *varṇa*s, the *varṇa*s are characterized by Śakti in essence, and Śakti should be known as *mātṛkā*, and *mātṛkā* should be known as the very

---

39. Vide C. Sivaramamurti, *Naṭarāja In Art Thought And Literature, op. cit.*, pp. 11-12.
40. H.N. Chakravarty, Mantra and the Significance of Sound, paper read in the National Seminar on Dhvani 11-14 March, 1999, *Jñāna Pravāha*, Varanasi. He says "*Prakāśa* which is translated as light is the very life of *artha*, object, while *vimarśa*, is self-awaring consciousness, the one is *vācaka* and the other is *vācya*."
41. *Ibid.*

essence of Śiva.[42] *Nāda* is thus the production of sound as well as the *bīja-rūpa, bindu.*[43]

For the seekers of the Ultimate Reality, the validity and the potency of the *mantra*s, the sacred syllabic sound, are of great importance. These *mantra*s may be meaningless sounds, words or sentences, but to the *sādhaka* (devotee) they become vibrant and potent and in the process do not merely remain sounds but translate/transform into visual images.[44] The artistic imagery of the *rāga-dhyāna* explains this thought amply. Taking the cue from this, the imagery may well be extended to the artistic movement in dance. *Nṛtta* (dance) is thus a visual representation of the manifestation of *nāda*, because the principles of composition are based on the immanent logic that governs any style of art, the basic law that determines its visual formulation. It may be abstract, but it is in fact a systematically defined cosmic conception. A reference to Śiva, revealing Himself as the great grammarian even as He dances and sounds the drum, is of great importance to bring home the point. A Paramāra inscription not only alludes to the Dancer but also explains the sound produced by Him on His drum, when as the Great grammarian, or the Lord of the science

42. H.N. Chakravarty, Mantra and the Significance of Sound, paper read in the National Seminar on Dhvani 11-14 March, 1999, *Jñāna Pravāha*, Varanasi.

43. Prem Lata Sharma, *The Alchemy of Love and Wisdom, op. cit.*, p. 117.

44. *Ibid.*, p. 104, wherein she explains : "Both modern physics and our traditional metaphysics of sound uphold that the objects of visual and auditory perception are not basically different, but are mutually convertible. It is common experience that hearing and seeing are not mutually supplementary or complementary, but are also capable of replacing each other to a considerable extent. The tradition of *rāga-dhyāna* was therefore nothing far-fetched or fantastic; it was a realistic approach to artistic imagery."

of language, he revealed the 14 Maheśvara *sūtras* to Pāṇini. These Maheśvara *sūtras* and the letters and *varṇas* are arranged in the *varṇa nāgakr̥pānika-bandha*. Interestingly, one of the dances of Śiva is known as the *Nādānta*.[45]

In the Hindu religious practice, the *sādhaka* (devotee) repeats the name of the deity in order to receive His blessings for the fulfilment of his desires.[46] In the religious parlance this is called *japa*.[47] With the constant repetition of the name of the deity, the devotee generates *spanda* (creative pulsation).[48] This is the *bindu* or the *Śiva-tattva*. The *bindu* is also called *ghaṇībhūta bindu*, i.e., the *bindu* is pregnant with all elements which constitute the totality of Manifestation. There is no *kriyā* (action/movement) without *spandana*, just as there is no movement without time and therefore no space without time and conversely no time without movement in space.[49] In the words of Padoux,

> Since the Vedic period, in spite of the superiority of the spoken word, the highest and the most efficacious form of that word, was not the loudest or the most intense, but on the contrary, the most silent and subtle — the inner utterance, the purely mental one. This is a fundamental trait of speech. . . . Indian Civilization . . . has more than any

---

45. See C. Sivaramamurti, *Naṭarāja In Art Thought And Literature, op. cit.*, pp. 136, 122.
46. On a grosser level we may understand the phenomenon in a more tangible or simpler way. The name of every individual by which they are addressed is a *mantra* of that individual. For only that individual responds to, or acts in the manner in which their name is taken.
47. *Japa* may be *mālā japa, upāṅgśu japa* (whispered utterance) or *mānasa japa* (mental).
48. Govindagopal Mukhopadhya, "Nāda in Spiritual Culture," paper read in the Seminar on Dhvani, infra.
49. Alice Boner, *Principles of Composition in Hindu Sculpture,* Cave Temple Period, Leiden, E.J. Brill, Netherlands, 1962, p. 14-20.

> other cultural area given to speech or word (*vāc*) a central, basic role and endlessly reflected upon it, studied it and considered it all powerful, the divine energy itself; this Civilization, in fact, has placed at the acme of speech, at the heart of every utterance, not sound but silence.[50]

It is often said that *nṛtta* (dance) is not all about movements, it is also equally related to or manifested with pauses. Mention has already been made to one of the dances of Śiva, the *Nādānta* (the cessation of all sound). Earlier I have also referred to a reference in the *Bhāgavata Purāṇa,* when the entire forest becomes *spandanahīna* as an effect of the strains from the flute of Kṛṣṇa. In fact, this is only a manifestation of the sequence of time and the division of space in all compositions of art whether painting or dancing.

> Space division and Time sequence, analytically differentiated, appear in all compositions, interwoven . . . like warp and woof on a loom. One is static and the other kinetic. The synthesis of both aspects and the meaning that results from it are . . . called Integration and Interpretation[51] (see *Pl.* 16, 17 also see *Pl.* 4 & 5).

In fact, Naṭarāja (Śiva) and Raṅganātha (Viṣṇu) also

---

50. Andre Padoux, *Mantras — What are they ? op. cit.*, p. 297, In the same book, Wheelock feels "while the Vedic liturgy uses language as a tool of proper action, the Tantra ritual makes action a subordinate of language in producing proper thought." Padoux however, stresses that there "certainly was an evolution from the Vedic to the Tantric attitude concerning the role of *mantras* in ritual, as tools of action or as thought producing or thought sustaining devices, nevertheless the admission of thought or consciousness as identical to the highest and silent level of speech is an ancient conception." same page.
51. Alice Boner, *Principles of Composition in Hindu Sculpture*, infra, see Preface also see, p. 245; also see C. Sivaramamurti, *Naṭarāja In Art Thought And Literature*, p. 36, *op. cit.*

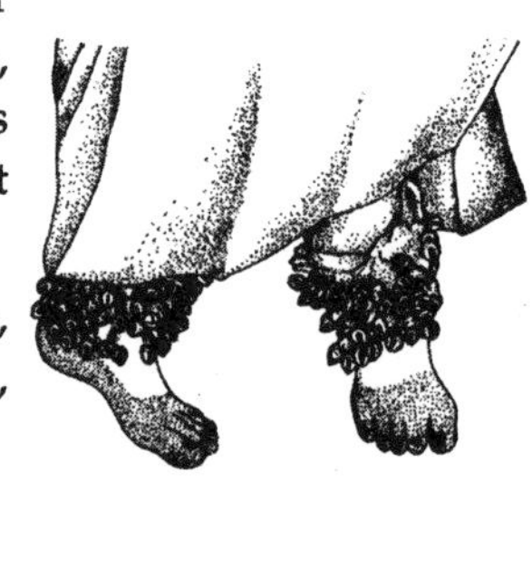

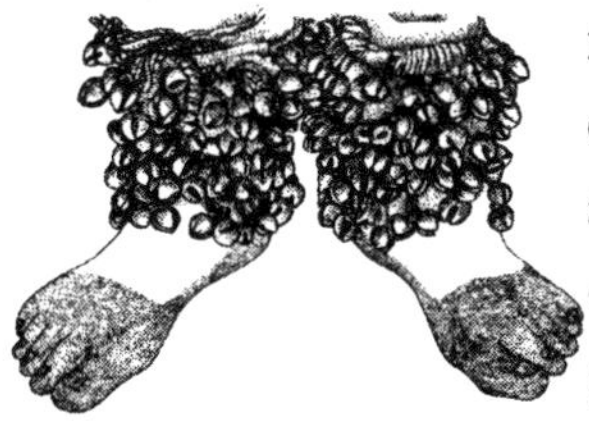

represent the dynamic and static aspects of identical concepts. The aphorism *nartaka ātmā* (the dancer is the supreme self) in the *Śivasūtravimarṣiṇī,* (3.9), refers to the dance of the Supreme Self, that suppresses its own real glorious form in *turīyāvasthā* by assuming the worldly roles in the state of awareness, sleep and dream (*jāgrat, suṣupti, svapna*), while Viṣṇu in *yoganidrā,* lying on the serpent couch on the waters, performs penance. It is for the ultimate good of the world. While Viṣṇu is ever active in sleep, Śiva, the *yogī* of *yogīs*, performs the dance of creation, protection and destruction (*sṛṣṭi, sthiti* and *saṁhāra*). This also explains the secret or the spiritual concept of *Guha,* which in its ultimate sense represents the cavern of the heart, the innermost centre of everything, where resides the *ātman* or *puruṣa. Guhas* (caverns) represent both death and resurrection. Death to the world and resurrection to the spirit.

Mantras, though related to the speech aspect of the humans, *vaikharī,* in fact, pass through the stages of *parā, paśyanti* and *madhyamā*. To achieve the desired end, a complete harmony between the mind, body and cosmos, they take recourse to *āsana* (body posture/position); *prāṇāyāma* (breathing exercise of the *iḍā, piṅgalā, suṣumanā*) and *dhyāna* (meditation) of which the final stage is *samādhi.* According to the Vedic *trica, nṛtya* is related to the body and there is predominance of *prāṇa, vādana* is related to the mind (*buddhi*) and there is predominance of *mana, gāyana* is related to the *hṛdaya* (heart) and there is predominance of *vāc*. Hindu *saṅgīta* is related both with the *Haṭha Yoga* (which deals largely with the body) and the *Rāja Yoga* (which is related with the *mānasa*). In *saṅgīta,* an effort is made to control the *vāc, prāṇa* and *mana* on all the levels, and so *saṅgīta* very easily becomes an adjunct to any *sādhana paddhati* (system), which uses the mind, body and *vāc* as its base. It is for this reason that in the *Śrībhaktirasāmṛtasindhu,* one of the *aṅgas* of *sādhana bhakti* is dance, referred to as *tāṇḍava*.[52] In ancient India, dance formed a part of all the important activities and functions, whether ritualistic or festivity celebrations : the *cūḍamāho utsava* (festival of the adoration of Siddhārtha's turban); the enlightenment as Buddha; the funeral celebration of Buddha at Kuśinagara, there was a general rejoicing celebrated with music and dance, as may be seen in the sculpture reliefs of the period[53] (see *Pl.* 18).

Mantras may have different forms and different uses. They are functional and different from ordinary speech. In the words of Padoux : "The inner organization of *mantras* and especially their phonetic structure are more important than their ordinary meaning, if any. They do not always say or mean what they seem to be saying," because perhaps *mantras* are a part of a ritual performance outside of which it is difficult to understand them.[54] *Nāṭya-Śāstra* (v. 102-106), refers to *stobhakriyā*, wherein it is stated that the feet movements of the dancer should be made to accompany the playing of drums. In this there is no song sung, but only the chant of meaningless syllables is prescribed. According to Bharata, *jhantum, jagatiya, valitak, titica* and such meaningless group of *varṇas* are called *śuśākakṣaras* or *vāc-karaṇas* and they reveal strong links both in time and space.[55] When *nāda* manifests in *vāc-karaṇas* in a definite time and space cycle or movement, it creates *laya* (rhythm)

52. Prem Lata Sharma, *The Alchemy of Love and Wisdom*, pp. 124, 117, *op. cit.*

53. C. Sivaramamurti, *Naṭarāja In Art Thought And Literature*, pp. 10-11, infra.

54. A. Padoux, *Mantras — What are they* ? infra.

55. *Nāṭya-Śāstra*, V. 102-6, p. 555, infra also see *Nāṭya-Śāstra*, 31-138, vide S. Choudhary, *Bhāratīya Saṅgīta Me Tāla Aur Rūpa Vidhānaha* (Hindi), Krishna Brothers, Ajmer, Rajasthan, 1984, pp. 305-12.

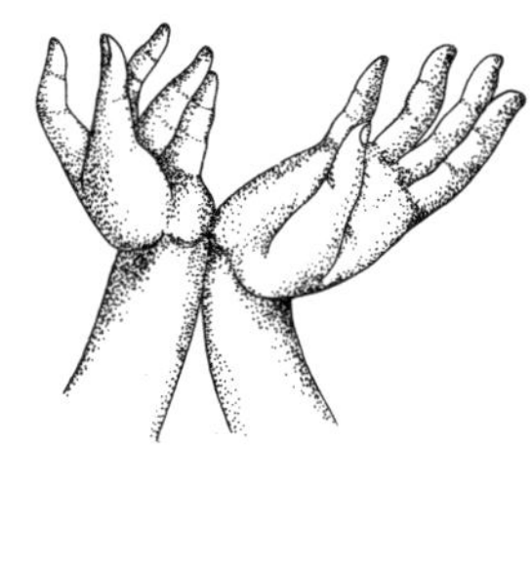

and *chanda* (metre). In *Kathaka* dance, the *bandishe*s (dance compositions) composed of apparently meaningless syllables are however recited in a particular way, with the correct pronunciation and punctuation. The term used to denote this process is *paḍhaṅta* (the *guru* or the dancer, beating time on the hands recites the *bol*s (mnemonic syllables), and there is a certain musicality in this verbal rendition of *bol*s. This phonetic or acoustic aspect of the composition is of great importance and should be taken up seriously, because though the mnemonic syllables do not have a meaning in the usual sense of the word or language yet they do have their efficacy, i.e., they do result in creating an effect, which is at times magical, in the sense that even for a short time the verbal or phonic form catches the attention of the users, the dancer as well as the audience/spectator who participate in the process, it transports them both to another level/ plane. This can be both postulative or intuitive. Such use of the acoustical resources of language has a magical effect. To quote Padoux,

> . . . it is nothing but a particular application of the symbolizing capacity of language, that is its capacity to represent something other than itself, to point towards something, whether an external referent or some inner meaning supposed inherent or to be identical with its phonic substance or to be some higher reality into which this substance eventually is supposed to dissolve.[56]

The manifestation of the *mantra* comes out at the level of the *vaikharī*, but in dance, the sound which is created by the dancer striking his feet on the ground or the physical movements of the body in space is in fact a transference of this *vaikharī*, which at the time of dancing is being silently repeated by the dancer in his *mānasa*. Even in the extempore sound productions by the feet, the dancer does verbalize

56. A. Padoux, *Mantras — What are they* ? p. 302-3, infra.

the rhythmic sound structure in his mouth/mind first at the level of *madhyamā*. The entire process is very quick and it requires the skill and maturity of artistic genius as well. The beauty of the rhythmic sound patterns created by the dancer are a result of his training, practise and insight into the grammar and the technicalities of his art, in our case *Kathaka*. The more sensitive and the more receptive the dancer is, the better patterns he will create. In other words, the quality of his "being" as a *pātra*, controls his level of artistry. Thus, though these meaningless mnemonic syllables may not have any literary value, yet they become vibrant and potent in the system of dance because they ultimately result in *Ānanda*.[57]

The repertoire of *Kathaka* reveals an abundance of such mnemonic *bols* and compositions, in the shape of *paraṇas*, *ṭukḍās*, *tatkāra*, *tihāī*, etc., etc. Under the *guru- śiṣya paramparā* much attention is paid to the *paḍhanta* (verbal recitation) aspect of the *bols*, which also include the *kākū prayoga*[58] (voice culture to produce quality sound). The effect of the recitation and the performance of the *bols/bandishes*

57. S. Choudhary, *Bhāratīya Saṅgīta Me Tāla Aur Rūpa Vidhānaha*, infra., pp. 305-12. Compare when she says that there is a social value even in the *chandas* in *nirarthaka padas*, because they give to the audience an experience of *ānanda*, also see. Kumbhā, Mahārāṇā, *Saṅgītarāja*, vol. I, p. 110, ed. Prem Lata Sharma, Nepal Rajya Sanskrit Series, vol. V, Hindu Vishvavidyalaya Sanskrit Pub. Board, Varanasi, 1963, where she says that *pāṭhya* is composed of syllabic sounds and is in fact a manifestation of *nāda*. "As for the presence or absence of suggestible meanings in sound (syllabic or non-syllabic) it may be said that there is no essential difference between the two, as both are equally powerful in their suggestive power (*vyañjanā śakti*). The difference lies only in the presence of primary meaning (*abhidhā śakti*) in syllabic sounds and the absence of that in non-syllabic ones. This means that syllabic sounds are more meaningful than non-syllabic ones."

58. *Kāku* is *dhvani* with tonal inflexions.

(compositions), is subject to the qualitative level of the dancer. If the dancer is a *sādhaka* and has achieved some level of *siddhi* (a yogic state) the performance works like magic. The mnemonic syllables/compositions are the *mantras* for this discipline. Just as a *mantra* is repeated thousands of time before it begins to vibrate and shine, the dancer repeats and practises the *bols*/compositions, hundreds of time to generate the dynamic divine radiant energy or else the purpose of dance as a *sādhanā* remains defeated. This is so because the mnemonic syllables are a part of a ritual performance, outside which they cannot really be understood and they have a meaning and value only within that ritual activity. For all this the dancer/*sādhaka* has to practise rigorously, with full devotion and complete conviction, all the *mudrās*, *sthānakas*, *carīs*, etc., along with the rhythmic mnemonic structure repeated first loudly and then repeated mentally (the mnemonics in the shape of *bols*/*bandishes*). This entire process as we see is akin to the *puraścaraṇa prakriyā* of *japa*.[59]

Many stories handed down by tradition supplement and amplify the powers inherent in *bols* and *bandishes* of *Kathaka* dance. I shall refer to a few as I have heard it from the mouth of my *guru* or other oral sources :

(1) Once a *Kathaka* dancer incurred the wrath of a Mogul Emperor and was ordered to be thrown before a mad elephant. The dancer (who it seems was perhaps a

59. H.N. Chakravarty, "Mantra and the Significance of Repetitive Sounds, Paper," *op. cit.*, wherein he says that for *puraścaraṇa* one should perform *japa* of the *mantra* for many hundred thousand times. . . . He also explains that the mental *japa* is performed in the level of the speech called *madhyamā*. The audible muttering of the *mantra* is done in such a way that it may be audible to the person who is engaged in the practice of *japa*. Both *upāṅgśu* and *saśabda* are done in the level of speech called *vaikharī* and both fulfil worldly benefits.

sādhaka) recited a *gaja paraṇa,*[60] when the elephant was let loose on him. The effect was such that the mad elephant sat down subdued before him.

(2) In the Hindu religious system, there are specific tonal productions through specific syllables for each deity.[61] These syllables are apparently meaningless but because of their specific vibrations and resonation, they arouse the *nāda,* which is the very soul of the *mantra,* to carry the *sādhaka/japaka* to his desired goal. In *Kathaka* also similar *akṣaras/varṇa*s are used to propitiate the deity. Such compositions are referred to as *Gaṇeśa paraṇas*, *Śiva paraṇa*s, *Durgā paraṇa*s, *Kālī paraṇa*s, etc. These compositions again very clearly show the impact and the interrelationship of the arts with the religious and spiritual culture of India. To give a few examples :

Gaṇeśa Paraṇa :

$_{+}$*Gaṅ Gaṅ* | $_{2}$*Gaṇapati* | $_{0}$*gaja mukha* | $_{3}$*maṇḍala* | $_{+}$*giṭa giḍa* | $_{2}$*giṭagiḍa* | $_{0}$*giṭa giḍa* | $_{3}$*thunthun* | $_{+}$*tat tat* | $_{2}$*thei* | $_{0}$*jai jaga* | $_{3}$*vandan* | $_{+}$*vakratu* | $_{2}$*nḍadā* | $_{0}$*nīdā* | $_{3}$*tā* | $_{+}$*vighna ha* | $_{2}$*rana sukha* | $_{0}$*karana dha* | $_{3}$*rana taka* | $_{+}$*dhimi kiṭa* | $_{2}$*dhimikiṭa* | $_{0}$*thuḍang* | $_{3}$*thuḍang* | $_{+}$*gadigina* | $_{2}$*thei thud* | $_{0}$*angthuda* | $_{3}$*angagadi* | $_{+}$*ginathei* | $_{2}$*thudang* | $_{0}$*thudang* | $_{3}$*gadigina* | $_{+}$*thei*

I bow to the Lord Gaṇapati, who has the face of an elephant, who rides the mouse, who has a crooked (turned) trunk, who is generous and remover of the obstacles, who dances and plays the *mṛdaṅga.*

---

60. *Gaja paraṇas* are special compositions composed of the *bols* from the *pakhāwaja* and they celebrate the various aspects of a *gaja* or elephant or even Lord Gaṇapati. Today only the names are left as many of the compositions of such rare beauty and qualification are lost or forgotten for reasons best known to everybody.

61. See the chapter on *Yantra.*

The mnemonic syllables used in *Śiva paraṇa*s are : *ḍima-ḍima, ḍimaka, dugata, ḍuga-ḍuga* (sound of the *ḍamaru*).

(3) It is also spoken by my *guru* that a *Kathaka* dancer (it is not clear whether any name of the dancer was given by my *guru* or it is some memory lapse on my part) would keep a full coconut on the ground before him. He would then recite the *bol*s and then perform it in the manner of *tatkāra* (footwork), and when the dancers feet struck the *sama* (starting and finishing point in the rhythmic cycle of *tāla*), the coconut would burst open ! Such were the vibrations created from the sound produced from the feet of the dancer striking the ground.

(4) Bindadin Maharaj is reported to have practised only *tatkāra* — *tā, thei, tata* and *tigadhā diga-diga* for nine years ! It is stated that when he performed the *tatkāra,* the vibrations created from the sound of the bells and the feet striking the ground, melted everyone's heart and the people experienced a joy in the magical sound of the bells.[62]

---

62. Bindadin was not just a doyen of *Kathaka,* he was a *sādhaka par excellence.* Even Coomaraswamy reports that once he saw Bindadin, an old man, singing and performing *abhinaya* on a *ṭhumarī.* Such was the transformation, that instead of an old man he saw a young sixteen year old *gopī* of Vṛndāvan. Such was the *siddhi* of Bindadin Maharaj. Vide A. Coomarswamy, *Rajput Painting,* Text, vol. I, Motilal Banarsidass, Varanasi, 2nd edn., 1976.

Ṭhumarī is a semi-classical form of Indian music. The lyrics in the *pada*s are saturated with the *śṛṅgāra rasa* (erotic sentiment). The *pada*s are *sārthaka* (meaningful). But though here we are concerned only with the *nirarthaka* (meaningless) syllables, the example is quoted to bring out the *siddhi* aspect in the dancer, Bindadin.

The mnemonics *tā, thei* and *tata* are the *bījākṣaras* of *Kathaka* dance as understood by the author. The production of the three different sounds by Viṣṇu as Trivikrama, with his feet hitting the three different elements of air, water and earth, brings into its ambit the metaphysics of the whole universe (see ch. on Yantra).

(5) Many more compositions, such as the *topa paraṇa* (cannon), the *baḍaiyā paraṇa* (carpenter); the *dal-bādal paraṇa* (clouds), suggestive of the central thought in the name itself, resonate the sound in the arrangement of the syllable structure. They are more secular in nature. According to Ashirvadam, such compositions may be called crypotrams. He makes an attempt in bestowing them with meaning, which has also been done earlier by other *gurus*.[63]

---

63. P.D. Ashirvadam, *Raigarh Darbar*, Agam Kala Prakashan, Delhi, 1990, pp. 161-62, wherein he refers to the compositions of Raja Cakradhara Singh, "We may call his compositions cryptograms, and cryptography is his dominant method of intensifying the effect. He ciphers the meaning and puzzles the reader by enigmatic use of meaningless syllables, in such a way that the sound units form a language of their own, which can easily be deciphered once the reader gets acquainted with the significance of sound syllables. Every now and then he suggests the meaning through clear cut sounds and guides the reader to reach the mysterious world of imagination." He further refers to it as the king's "own argot of meaningless syllables," and records an analytical study of the same :

    Kilkila-Paraṇa of Raja Cakradhara Singh in *tritāla*

    $_+$*Dhe theṭa gheghe tiṭa* | $_2$*taḍa.............ga* |
    $_0$*thā – katha-ka gheghe* | $_3$*gheghe gheghe dhum maka* | |

    $_+$*dhage din gana dhage* | $_2$*din gana gheti tata* |
    $_+$*gedi gana trika tata* | - $_3$*na trika tata-na* | |

→

We may thus conclude that the mnemonic syllables of *Kathaka*, though apparently meaningless, are loaded with power — the power of *Nāda-Brahman*. The *Saṅgīta Darpaṇa*, an ancient treatise, discusses the *sapta-svaras* in relation to *nṛtya* (dance). *Śrīkaṇṭha-carita* (1.35) expresses the same thoughts beautifully; even Sarasvatī, the goddess not only

---

→ $_{+}$*dhara nami – na dhet* | $_{2}$*dhaḍa – nna dha.........* |
$_{0}$*kiḍtak ta dingaḍ dha* | $_{3}$*dhakid takta dignaḍ dha* | |

$_{+}$*gheghe tita tage - nna* | $_{2}$*dha........ gheghe tiṭa* |
$_{0}$*taga — nna dha ....* | $_{3}$*gheghe tita taga – nna.*
$_{+}$*dha* | |

Ashirvadam explains :

First line : *tete* suggest *tat*, i.e., the bank of a river or lake, *taḍāga* means lake. 1. therefore means on the banks of a lake (a bird).

Second line : *tak* means *takna*, i.e. to look this side and that side with keen interest. It, therefore, means that the bird looked this side and that side keenly with the interest to catch a fish. The second half of the second line beautifully expresses the subtle jerks in the neck movement of the heron or *kilkila* bird.

The third and fourth lines : portray the movements of the small fish in water, which swim hither and thither, even near the feet of the heron, unaware of their fatal end. The *bols* in these lines suggest the swift turns of the fish and their graceful forward movement. *Trik* is for the swift turn and *tatana* is for the forward movement.

The fifth line : *dharan meen* means the catch of the bird. Hence the line means : the heron caught the fish with a sudden splash and flew away.

The sixth line : depicts the killing of the fish, on the branch of a tree by the beak of the bird. "the gulping, munching and final swallowing is beautifully depicted in the *tihāī*. He sums up thus : "A small lake or pond with some small fish in its crystal clear water, a big tree on its bank; a crane or heron standing like a pious man on the edge of the bank, without even the slightest movement as if in deep meditation. Small and innocent fish dancing in front of it. At a proper moment it catches one of them with a sudden splash; flies away, and →

of learning and music but also of dance (since the *Gandharvaveda* includes dance), is approached by a fleet of swans attracted by the sound of her anklets, the jingling of which resembles the sweet warble of the birds, as she skillfully dances on the tongues of poets, which is the *vācika*

→ sits on the branch of a tree comfortably, and munches and swallows it. The whole picture comes so vividly to the connoisseur's mind that the "composition becomes crystal clear in spite of its cryptic nature."

Similarly there is one *parmelu* (compositions/*bandiśas* composed from mnemonics/*bols* from various sources) which the author had learnt during her early years of training. The movements and the mnemonics have today acquired a more meaningful metaphysical outlook, as we shall see in an analytical study of the same :

$_{+}$*Drigajhagi* | $_{2}$*radrigajha* | $_{0}$*girajhaga* | $_{3}$*jhagataka* | $_{+}$*takathira* | $_{2}$*kajhagena* |

$_{0}$*jhagataka* | $_{3}$*kukutigadhadizadiga* | $_{+}$*theitaka* | $_{2}$*kukutigadhadigadiga* |

$_{0}$*theitaka* | $_{3}$*kukutigadhadigadiga* | $_{+}$*thei*

Dṛga means eyes, its symbolical meaning is looking.

Jhagira means *jhānkanā* or peeping.

Taka means looking.

Thirakana means dancing.

Kuku means bird.

Tigadhadigadiga expresses the flying movement of the bird.

The dance movements of the composition shows a girl looking at herself in the mirror, dancing in admiration of her youth and beauty, with her soul rising high in joy as the soaring high of the *kuku* bird. On the metaphysical plane the same composition could reveal more depth into the apparently secular appearance of the composition. The composition would then mean that a girl, watching and admiring her youth and beauty in the mirror, realizes that it is only an illusion and that the truth is the ephemeral nature of all things which will one day fly-away into oblivion just as the flying away of the *kuku* bird.

part of *abhinaya*.[64] Thus, the power which is ultimately revealed, has to be realized by the dancer through a correct rendering of the *bols*, through regular and correct practise, because it is ultimately an expression of *vāc*. The rendering of the *bols* in dance is through *abhinaya* (*āṅgika, vācika, āhārya* and *sāttvika*) expressed through the various movements of the body. The *Japasūtram* which explains the science and the metaphysics of *japa*, is largely devoted to an understanding of the metaphysics of sound from the various stages of *parā, paśyanti, madhyamā* and *vaikharī* — the root by which sound converts itself into light, then into physical sound and ultimately into physical form.[65] Thus, the *rūpa* or form in dance is in fact the evolution and the manifestation of the sound-energy (the *Tantra-Śāstra* very clearly states that every form is a product of sound) and though abstract and obstruse, it is in fact fundamental objectivation of the spiritual image of our universe and therefore important in moulding the specific inimitable character of the traditional art form — *Kathaka*. It is only the artist who as a *sādhaka* translates the mystery of the world into the mystery of Form. Just as for the efficacy of the sacred word, *mantra*, correct pronunciation, intonation, pitch and metre are important, so also, is their importance in the production of the mnemonic syllables of *Kathaka* dance, the roots for both being common.

64. P.D. Ashirvadam, *Raigarh Darbar*, Agam Kala Prakashan, Delhi, 1990, pp. 112-13. *Saṅgīta Darpaṇa* is not published. The material for the *Nartan-Sarvasvam* (book not available), according to Ashirvadam, is derived from the *Saṅgīta Darpaṇa*. Also see Sivaramamurti, *Nataraja in Art Thought and Literature*, p. 71, *op. cit.* for the reference of *Śrīkaṇṭhacarita*.

65. *Japasūtram*, vide M.P. Pandit, *Studies in the Tantras and the Veda*, Sterling Publishers, New Delhi, 1988, p. 46.

3

Yantra

In the Hindu system, the body has been the subject of study not only of physicians, doctors and scientists, but also of philosophers, sages and musicians. It is for this reason that books on philosophy, religion or *saṅgīta* contain chapters or sections devoted to the study of the human body : its anatomy, physiology, psychology along with its spiritual and metaphysical dimensions, i.e., the body possessed of *caitanya*. The most beautiful and intriguing part of this study is that in the final stage they all merge into one.[1] Thus, in the Hindu system, *saṅgīta* is very greatly influenced by religion and it thus becomes a *sādhanā*, while religion becomes a subject of study for the philosophers. Though

---

1. A. Mukherjee, *Tantra Art : Its Philosophy and Physics*, Ravi Kumar, New Delhi, 1971, p. 13, wherein he says ". . . In this way the Tantric rituals are the basis of many a philosophy, Śaiva, Śākta, Jaina, Buddhist or Vaiṣṇava. . . Also see "Influence of Tantra on Music," in S.C. Banerji, *Fundamentals of Ancient Indian Music and Dance*, L.D. Institute of Indology, Ahmedabad, 1976, wherein he says, "The use of *mudrā*s or positions of hands, etc., in connection with *saṅgīta*, particularly with dance, seems to testify to Tāntric influence. The idea of *mudrā*s as symbolizing feelings, moods, sentiments, etc., probably originated in the Vedic period. In Vedic rituals, various poses were adopted by the singer of *sāman*s. The *mudrā*s, however, along with the mystical diagrams called *maṇḍala* and *yantra* were highly developed in connection with the Tāntric rites. It may be that with the diffusion of Tāntric rites the *mudrā*s came to be included in a large number of works on music."

the approach is holistic and the aim is the same : the realization of the Absolute, the state of *Saccidānanda,* yet the ways and methods employed are different (though many a times overlapping) and for this reason each discipline maintains its own autonomy.

One of the ways of realizing and experiencing this eternal bliss is through the worship of the *yantra*. As commonly understood, *yantra* means an instrument, which is used to accomplish something. In the *Tantra-Śāstra* the *yantra* is a diagram engraved or drawn on metal, paper or skins of specific animals or even human bones and is worshipped as a substitute of image worship (*pratimā-pūjana*), along with the *uccāraṇa* (utterance) of specific *mantras*. According to the Jaina *Divyāvadāna*, an image or a *yantra* is a piece of psychological apparatus to call up one or the other aspects of divinity.[2] The ritualistic, allegorical and symbolical interpretation of the *yantra* may be seen as far back as the *Śatapatha Brāhmaṇa* (3.6.4.27) and the *Aitareya Brāhmaṇa* (1.6.1) where *yūpas* (sacrificial posts) are stated to be the symbol of the *vajra* (thunder- bolt), which is stated to be eight-sided (octagonal). This example also suggests some kind of relationship between symbol and the beauty of form, as forms have a more lasting impression on the human mind (*mānasa*).[3] Giving another dimension to the relationship, Kramrisch points to the reference in the *Aitareya Brāhmaṇa* (6.5.27), where it is stated, "Śilpani, works of art of man are an imitation of divine forms; by employing their rhythms, a metrical reconstruction is effected of the limited human personality."[4] Even Bharata,

2. A. Mukherjee, *Tantra Art : Its Philosophy and Physics*, Ravi Kumar, New Delhi, 1971, p. 13.
3. M.N. Joshi, *Art and Science in Mānsollasa*, New Bharatiya Book Corporation, Delhi, 2003.
4. Stella Kramrisch, *Exploring India's Sacred Art*, ed. Barbara Stoler Miller, Philadelphia, 1983, p. 60.

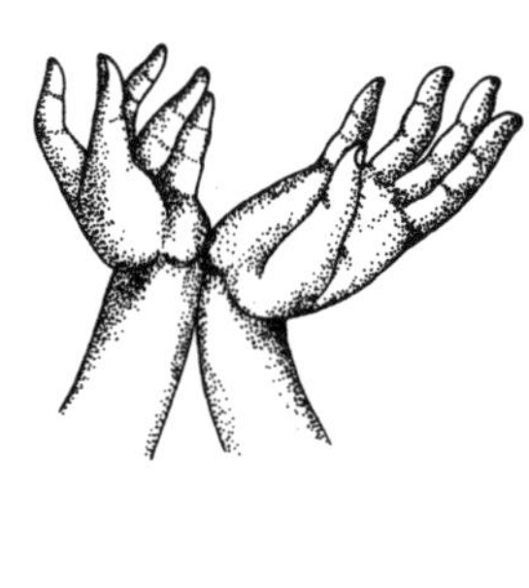

the author of *Nāṭya-Śāstra*, Chs. I and II, may be seen as contemplating upon the thoughts and the rituals of the Upaniṣads and the *Brāhmaṇas* by establishing relationship of the physical (gross) to the psychical (subtle) and the metaphysical (beyond) on the one hand and the limited physical space being made into a symbolic design just like forming the *vedikā* of the *yajña* in the Vedas and on the other hand considering those who perform not as particular individual's portraying subjective emotions but as single entities who represent part of an organic whole.[5]

Daṇḍī in the *Kāvyād* (11.260), states that representation of the beautiful in art is a complex process involving a number of processes — some of them are gross while others are subtle. He says, when the meaning is indicated delicately

---

5. Vide "Manifestation of Nature, Sṛṣṭi Vistāra,"in *Kalātattavakośa*, vol. IV, IGNCA, 1994, p. 314; also see p. 301, where it says that in Tantra, the gross, subtle and the transcendent have been viewed with reference to means (*upāya*) for the removal of misery of the worldly existence. The *Netra Tantra* states that the means of getting rid of misery are three, viz., *sthūla, sūkṣma* and *parā*. "The means for its attainment is threefold. It is gross, subtle and transcendent. But the gross is the offering to the deity, oblation into the fire, repetition of the *mantra*, meditation (of the deity) along with *mudrā*s. But the subtle one is performed with the association of *cakra*s and so on, and by means of getting the minute time units (*kalā*s) to rise along the principal channels (inside the body and then they should be impelled to move upwards). The transcendent is all-pervading," *Netra Tantra*, VI. 6 cd-7ab, 8abc; also see p. 315 where it states that though the terms *sthūla, sūkṣma* and *parā* may seem as distinct concepts at the phenomenal level or plane, but it is only an aspirant, a real aesthete, or a *sahṛdaya*, who alone can perceive these concepts as emerging from the same source; also see pp. 311, 302, 303 where it explains that the process of *mantra* and *mudrā* though starts at the *sthūla* or gross level, it ultimately rises to merge in the subtle and finally in the transcendent.

by gesture and *ākāra* (or the condition of the body), then it is considered to be *sūkṣma*. Thus the basis of all forms of Indian art or creativity, whether poetry, sculpture, music or dance, may be found in the thoughts of the

> Upaniṣads or the rituals of the *Brāhmaṇas*, because the basic nature and the manifestation of each form is in fact an expression of the Ultimate. Reality as it is understood at its grossest level, which it again transcends to become universal or transcendent/*parā* (i.e., beyond the gross and the subtle), . . . the gross and the subtle are the modes through which the identification of the transcendent with the form is attained. Because the artistic creation is an embodiment of this entity in a gross form, what is subtle in it is only an object of perception. Keeping this in mind, the art may be defined as the refined and sophisticated skill of creating a new world through any particular artistic medium such as literature, sculpture, architecture, music and dance.[6]

It is only the really devoted artist, a *sādhaka* (a real aspirant) or a *sahṛdaya* (a real aesthete), who is able to perceive these apparently different concepts and forms as emerging from the same source. Boner also holds a similar view when she says that the figural compositions refer to mysteries, spiritual events, descent of divine forces into the cosmos. Their composition on a foundation of cosmic and spiritual symbolism maintains the spiritual perspective and in spite of its anthropomorphic garb, prevents their transcendent reality from shrinking to purely human dimension.[7]

The process of creation in the *Tantra-Śāstra* finds expression in form in the various icons as well as in the various rarefied diagrammatic or graphic designs, referred

6. Vide "Manifestation of Nature, Sṛṣṭi Vistāra," *Kalātattavakośa*, vol. IV, IGNCA, 1994, *Kalātattavakośa*, vol. IV, p. 313.
7. Alice Boner, *Principles of Composition in Hindu Sculpture, Cave Temple Period*, Leiden, E.J. Brill, Netherlands, 1962, p. 30.

to as *yantras*. To understand the real nature of the *yantras*, "one has to go beyond the notions of geometry into those of dynamics. A *yantra* then represents particular forces whose power of energy increases in proportion to the abstraction and precision of the diagram. . . . Through such a *yantra* or power diagrams creation and control of ideas and physical forces are supposed to be possible."[8] The *yantra,* thus, though apparently a graphic design is in fact a visual form/representation of the visual world as well as its energies which are operative at various levels of consciousness : abstract as well as physical, both within the individual as well as the "invisible world" within the physical world that we know. The macrocosm is thus represented as the *Vāstu Puruṣa Maṇḍala* or the *Dhanurveda Puruṣa*, or the *Āyurveda Puruṣa* or the *Saṅgīta Puruṣa*, according to the particular *Upaveda* or *vidyā* predicated to him.

Symbols have played an important role in the religious, spiritual, artistic and even secular nature of the Indian culture. They not only give form and meaning to the thoughts within the mind but in a reverse manner they prove their effectiveness by taking the mind from the outside to the inside and though they have a *finite* form they have the potential to suggest the formless *infinite.* The abstract or

---

8. A. Mukherji, *Tantra Art — Its Philosophy and Physics, op. cit.* p. 20, also see Kumbhā, Mahārāṇa, vol. I, ed. Prem Lata Sharma, Hindu Vishvavidyalaya Sanskrit Pub. Board, 1963, p. 72, for names of the four Upavedas and their respective Vedas :

   आर्युर्वेदं धनुर्वेदं गान्धर्व वेदमात्मनः।

   स्थापत्यं चासृजद्वेदं क्रमात्पूर्वादिभिर्मुखैः।। (*Bhāg*, 3.12.38).

   तत्र वेदानामुपवेदाश्चत्वारो भवन्त्यृग्वेदस्यायुर्वेद उपवेदो यजुर्वेदस्य धनुर्वेद उपवेदः ।

   सामवेदस्य गान्धर्ववेदोऽथर्ववेदस्यार्थशास्त्रं चेत्याह भगवान्व्यासः।।

   — चरणव्यूहपरिशिष्टभाष्ये चतुर्थी कण्डिका, पृ० 47

the esoteric nature of the symbols is thus only a control and the manipulation of the psychological and the physical energy. Symbols such as the *bhaṅgīs*, *mudrās* (poses and gestures) *āsanas* are common to *yoga*, *tantra*, the visual/ performing arts such as painting, sculpture, the art of dance, because they are imitative in nature and representative of the objects of the three worlds.[9] The *yantra*, as a symbol of the microcosmic representation of the entire visible world makes use of the basic principles of mathematics and geometry, in the imagery of the *bindu*, the line, the square, the triangle, the pentagon, the hexagon, etc.[10] The *yantra*,

---

9. Bharata Muni, *Nāṭya-Śāstra* 1.118-119; 1.112; 1.107, with commentaries *Abhinavbhāratī, Madhūsūdani, Bālakrīḍā*, BHU, Varanasi 1971, see pp. 141, 131-32, 109.

   Lokavṛttnukaraṇama nāṭyametanmaya kṛtam, 112, and *Trailokyasyāsya sarvasya nāṭyam bhavānukirtanam*, 107; also see *V.Dh. Purāṇa*, 35.5, ed. Priyabala Shah, Oriental Institute, Baroda, 1958.

   Yathā nṛtte tathā citre trailokyanukṛtiḥ smṛtaḥ, 5.

10. Philip Rawson, *Tantra*, Thames & Hudson, London, 1973, p. 15 wherein the scholar states : "if we recognize that all our universe in time emerges through psychosomatic forces, then we can symbolize these forces by images of men and women possessed by them. But Tantra art also uses a variety of extremely rarefied diagrammatic *yantras* (*Pls.* 4-6). It would be easy to call these abstract, but this however would be wrong. These symbols refer to something denser and more real than everyday world, they convey energy realities which are so inclusive and emotionally exciting as to go far beyond the limit of ordinary objects we can recognize from everyday experience." Also see M.N. Joshi, *Art and Science in Mansollasa, op. cit.*, p. 83, wherein the relationship between *vāstu* and its symbolism is explained, "*Maṇḍala* denotes any closed polygon. The square which is the essential form of any *Vāstu-Puruṣa* can be converted into a triangle, hexagon, octagon and circle of equal area and retain its symbolism." Also see Stella Kramrsich, *Exploring Indian's Sacred Art, op. cit.*, p. 62, wherein she talks of symbolic diagram, "It is the

→

however, only becomes powerful with the ritual of the *mantra*, which includes *homa, japa, prāṇa-pratiṣṭhā* (infusion of life and vitality), etc.[11]

The *yantra* as a diagrammatic/geometric representation also makes a conscious use of space. According to the *Chāndogya Upaniṣad*, everything originates and finally dissolves in space.[12] According to the *Śatapatha Brāhmaṇa* space is contained in the concept of *bhū* (*pṛthvī*). The art form which is most directly connected with the *bhū*/earth/ space is architecture, though the arts of painting, sculpture, dancing make ample use of space as well. *Ākāśa* also denotes empty space, both in the unlimited firmament as well as

---

→ diagram of existence here on earth. In its symmetry and proportion are stationed all the powers that are active in the cosmos and in man. The meaning is explained by its myth. It is a kind of module."

11. The Kaulavalī states that the soul of the *yantra* is the *mantra* and the soul of the *mantra* is the deity which is potentialized in a condensed form in the *bījākṣara* (seed syllable) which is its verbal form of manifestation, "From the seed syllable the *mantra* evolves. All extensions terminate in a point and all verbalizations dissolve in a seed syllable; and all thoughts end in the deity. There is thus a correspondence between the deity, central point, seed syllable. There is also a correspondence between the *mantra, yantra* and the dimensions of the devotee consciousness." vide S. Ramachandra Rao, *Yantra*, Sri Satguru Publications, Delhi 1988, p. 24.

12. *Chāndogya Upaniṣad*, Wherefrom do all these worlds come ? They come from space. All beings arise from space and into space they return : space is indeed the beginning and space is their final end. The *Taittirīya Upaniṣad* also speaks in a similar way : From space came air, from air came fire. From fire came water. From water came solid earth. From earth come living plants. From plants — food and seed, and from food and seed come a living being: man, vide Nik Douglas, *Tantra Yoga, op. cit.*, p. 33.

the inner, not less limited space of the heart.[13] The stage where drama is enacted or dance performed is in fact a bounded space on the *bhūmi* (earth). The *Nāṭya-Śāstra* treats the *bhūmi* at three levels :

(i) At the physical level, where it means the earth or ground of the stage or auditorium.

(ii) At the physio-psychological level, where it means the level of the perception of space by the audience.

(iii) At the psycho-aesthetic level, where it involves the actors in the presentation of dramatic episodes.

In all the three levels, the thread of unity is that *bhūmi* or *bhūmikā* is the ground on which a physical construction, perceptional creation or aesthetic presentation is based.[14]

---

13. *Kalātattavakośa,* vol. II, (1992) infra. There is also a reference to *mahākāśa, ghaṭākaśa, cidākaśa* and *bṛnayākāśa,* in the macrocosmic, microcosmic, mental and spiritual sense; also see *Kalātattavokośa,* vol. III, (1996), infra, p. 365.

14. *Kalātattavakośa,* vol. II, p. 397, wherein it is stated that the *bhūmi* also signifies different planes of spiritual development in Buddhist or other systems of *yoga.* It is the firm ground on which the physical and spiritual realities stand and it also plays a very important role in cosmology as well as soteriology. Also see p. 391, wherein the ritual importance of *bhūmi-kṣetra,* is emphasized, and the analogy is taken to explain the extension of the concept in *yantra.* It says, "The same idea is depicted in cosmograms like the *śrīyantra,* which symbolizes the universe as the temple of the sovereign Goddess. Also see *Kalātattavakośa,* vol. III, 1996, infra., wherein it explains, "Since creative activity and all the art forms imitate the process of creation, the concept of space, the first created principle, is the very basis on which artistic creation proceeds. Emptiness is the prerequisite for the manifestation of name and form. The geometric form that represent the *ākāśa* in the Tantras is the circle that symbolizes the totality of creation. Fullness and expansion along with the connotations of space permeate the arts. Art represents

→

Along with *space*, the art of *saṅgīta* (music and dance) also makes a clever use of time as rhythm (*laya/tāla*). Space naturally takes within its ambit the concept of time. All movements take place in time and space. There is thus no movement without time and therefore, no space without time and conversely no time without movement in space.

> The basic concepts of culture acquire meaning only when seen against the background of cosmology, its understanding of space and time. These concepts determine the concrete symbolic forms of the Arts.[15]

Viṣṇudharamottara Purāṇa also declares the close connection between the art of *Vāstu-Śāstra* and the science of *citra* and dance. In fact, the *Vāstu-Śāstra* often included the science of *Citra-Śāstra* and the art of *nṛtta*.[16] Bharata specifically refers to the decoration of the walls of the *raṅga-maṇḍapa* (theatre) with beautiful paintings and sculptures.[17] The design of the *nāṭya-maṇḍapa* according to Viśvakarmā, as stated by Bharata, being *vikṛṣṭa, caturasra* and *trayasra* (rectangle, square and triangle) and its worship through rituals and *mantras* clearly suggests

---

→ on the material level the concept of space as the model of microcosmic and macrocosmic relationships, the unity of inner and outer space." Also see *Saṅgītaratnākara*, vol. I, 1.2.12-15, tr., R.K. Shringy and Prem Lata Sharma, Munshiram Manoharlal, New Delhi, 1992, p. 32, "From *ātman* emanated ether, first of all, followed by air, fire, water, and earth in their respective order." These are again dissolved back into the *Brāhmana* in the cycle of creation and dissolution.

15. *Ibid., Kalātattavakośa*, vol. II.

16. *Viṣṇudharamottara Purāṇa*, 35.5, infra,

    grahyamasa sa tada viśvakarmarḍamacyutam
    yathā nṛtte tathā citre trailokyanukṛtiḥ smṛtaḥ
    — 11.5

17. Bharata Muni, *Nāṭya-Śāstra* (2.80-90) with commentaries *Abhinavabhāratī, Madhusūdanī, Bālakrīḍā, op. cit.*, pp. 188-191.

the formation of a *yantra*, possessed of *caitanya*.[18] The Orissan *śilpa* text, *Śilpa Prakāśa*, lays down rules for preparing a *tāṇḍava yantra*, on which the *nṛtta mūrti*s are to be shown, because it is believed that the dance image of Śiva increases bliss.[19] *Yātrāprabandha* of Samarapungava Dikshita clearly states

> . . . dance is the one means of attaining all desired objects by sentient beings and the art of dance is this. Is it not in this spirit O Lord of Puṇḍarīkaputra that you dance to show the mode of dance movements ?[20]

Sound is also one of the qualities of space and though space is the first element to emanate from the Supreme self, *Brahman*,

---

18. *Ibid.*, 2.79, p. 96, wherein Brahmā requests Viśvakarmā to build a *nāṭyaśālā* which is *lakṣaṇasampanna; NŚ* 2.83-98, Brahmā requests the deities, *devatā*s to take their appropriate place in the *raṅgaśālā* : the moon to take care of the entire *maṇḍapa*, the *lokapāla*s to keep a watch over the four directions, Vāyu for all the *diśā*s (directions), Sūrya to take care of the *nepathya bhūmi* (green-room), Varuṇa to stay in the *ambara* (sky, here upper region of the *raṅgaśālā*), Agni to take care of the *vedī* (sacred place), and other *devatā*s to take care of *bhāṇḍa* (instruments), the four *varṇa*s to take their places in the four pillars; Āditya and Rudras also were to take care of the other pillars; *bhūta*s to take their place in the garters and *apsarā*s to take care of the *śālā*s (the rooms in the upper story) and the list goes on for every nook and corner to be occupied by *yakṣiṇī*s, *nāga*s, etc., etc. In the centre of the *raṅgapīṭha* Brahmā himself took position; *NŚ* (2.46-63), refers to the rituals, the *mantra* to be performed at the correct time/ hour, for auspiciousness and blessings; *NŚ* (1-8), explicitly states that worship of the stage is akin to a *yajña; NŚ* (2.7-8), refers to the three basic designs of the *nāṭya-maṇḍapa*, and their three sizes.
19. Vide C. Sivaramamurti, *Naṭarāja In Art Thought and Literature*, Publications Division, Ministry of Information and Broadcasting, Govt. of India, New Delhi, 1994, p. 144.
20. *Ibid.*, p. 370.

the actual creation takes place through the word.[21] *Brahman* is also known as *Virāj*, which literally means luminous, splendour. It is believed that *Brahman* having created the five elements, entered into them.[22] The *Śrīmad Bhāgawata* (I.1.23), states that

> *Brahman* may suitably be called "space" (*ākāśa*) because being of the nature of light, it shines (*ākāśate*) by itself and makes other things shine forth (*ākāśyati*). This is because the nature of *Brahman* is *prakāśa* (effulgence) and there is an invariable relationship between light and space.[23]

The concept of space (*ākāśa*) includes the concept of *diśā* (direction) though unlike *ākāśa*, it is not regarded as an element.[24] *Saṅgītaratnākara* states that the body as a composite of the five great elements (earth, water, fire, air and ether) acquires their qualities: sound, the faculty of hearing, porosity, individuation, intelligence and hollowness from space and touch, the sense-organ of touch, five types of motion, viz., upwards, downwards, contraction, linear and expansion from air, roughness and lightness are also derived from air; from fire the body acquires, sight, luster, wrath, sharpness, vigour, splendour, valour, intellectuality, etc., from water, the body drives, taste, relish, coolness, viscidity, fluidity, softness, etc.,

---

21. *Saṅgītaratnākara*, vol. I, *op. cit.*, p. 34. The creation takes place through the word, as codified in the Vedas. The Vedas in the Indian tradition are considered to be *apauruṣeya*, i.e., literally beyond human authorship. Since creation and dissolution in the author's view form a unitary movement, the creation takes place through the word of the Vedas, which through the process of association give rise to the form as ideas in the universal mind, which then creates the world according to those ideas, the latent seeds." Also see *Saṅgītaratnākara*, 1.2.14-15, *Ibid.*, wherein it states : "However, in essence *ākāśa* means that objective reality, which is the substratum of sound perceived by the ear.
22. *Ibid*, p. 32.
23. Vide *Kalātattvakośa*, vol. III, *op. cit.*
24. *Chāndogya Upaniṣad*, VII. 25, vide *Kalātattavakośa*, vol. III, *Ibid.*

from earth the body acquires, smell odour, stability, fortitude, heaviness, hair, bones, etc.[25] *Bṛhaddeśī* clearly states that the combination of air with fire (*māruta* and *vahni*) gives birth to *nāda*, from which all *vāṅgmaya* (whatever is made of speech or language) is born. *Vahni* (fire) arises from *prāṇa* seated in the *Brahma-granthī* (point of navel), which is the *sthāna* (location) of Brahmā.[26]

Thus, the interrelationship of the various elements on different planes plays an important role in the evolution and expression of the arts, in our case dance. *Vāyu* implies both movement and dynamism. It is responsible both for the production of sound in *saṅgīta*, and as a symbol of dynamism, it is the principle element in the movement of dance and sculpture. *Ṛgveda*, describes the dynamic play of the winds as the dance of the Maruts and praises its nature as moving swiftly in different directions,[27] and because of this association of the wind with the playful movement of dance, Abhinavagupta praises the wind form, *Samīramūrti* of Śiva in his benedictory verse in the *Abhinavabhāratī*.[28]

The *yantra*, thus, as a *citra* (diagrammatical/geometrical) with the power of the *mantra*, not only embodies space but is also empowered with the various cosmological energies

25. *Saṅgītaratnākara*, 1.2,56-70, infra, pp. 57-58.

26. *Bṛhaddeśī*, Kalāmulaśāstra Series (8), pp. 6-7, ed. Prem Lata Sharma, A.B. Beohar, IGNCA, Delhi, 1992.

27. Vide *Kalātattavakośa*, vol. II, *op. cit.*, p. 176.

28. *Nāṭya-Śāstra*, IV.1 infra p. 222, For the translation also see *Kalātattavakośa* vol. III, p. 182, infra, it reads : "I worship the aerial body of the lover of the daughter of the king of the mountains who constantly manifests the universe by his playful movements;" also see pp. 123, 176, wherein it is stated that one of the names of Viṣṇu is Vāyu. The *Viṣṇu Purāṇa* (1.14.32) states that space (*ākāśa*) is the body of Viṣṇu. It is also an attribute of the deity. The conch in Viṣṇu's hand symbolizes *kha*, the symbol of space, and hence his mastery over the celestial sphere.

bestowed from the basic five elements which constitute the cosmos. The movements in dance as an expression of the human body are in fact the manifestations of the sound-energy as evolved in a *rūpa* (form) (we have already seen how according to *Tantra-Śāstra* every form is a product of sound).[29] The body, thus, as a *yantra* represents the field of consciousness (*citta*), the mnemonic syllables of dance as the vocalized formula for repetition, representing the expressive faculty of consciousness, *vac* manifests the *mantra*, and the *mudrās* in dance, performed as physical postures and gestures represent the material vehicle in which consciousness is embodied and through which it works. This symbolism and philosophy to a large extent is a result of the influence of Tantra on dance and thus an important factor in any consideration or evaluation of ancient Indian music and dance.[30]

29. *Bṛhaddeśī*, 1.12, Kalāmūlaśāstra Series (8), *op. cit.*, pp. 4-5, "Dhvani is the ultimate origin (*yoni*, lit. womb), *dhvani* is the cause of everything. The whole world of immobile and mobile (beings) is encompassed by *dhvani* (12), also see *Bṛhaddeśī*, 1.18, "There is no *gīta* (song, music) without *nāda*, there are no *svara*s (musical notes) without *nāda*, there is no *nṛtta* (dance) without *nāda*, hence the world is of the essence of *nāda* (18).

30. S.C. Banerji, "Influence of Tantra on Music," in *Fundamentals of Ancient Indian Music and Dance*, L.D. Series 57, L.D. Institute of Indology, Ahmedabad 1976, says: The use of *mudrās* or positions of hands, etc., in connection with *saṅgīta*, particularly with dance, seems to justify Tāntric influence. The idea of *mudrās*, as symbolizing feelings, moods, sentiments, etc., probably originated in the Vedic period. In Vedic rituals, various poses of hands were adopted by the singer of *sāmans*. The *mudrās* however, along with the mystical diagrams called *maṇḍala* and *yantra*, were highly developed in connection with the tāntric rites. It may be that with the diffusion of tāntric rites, the *mudrā* came to be included in a large number of works on music. Also see Douglas, Nik, *Tantra Yoga*, Munshiram Manoharlal, New Delhi, 1971, p. 65, wherein he also expresses similar thoughts: breath-movement (*prāṇāyāma*) is closely related →

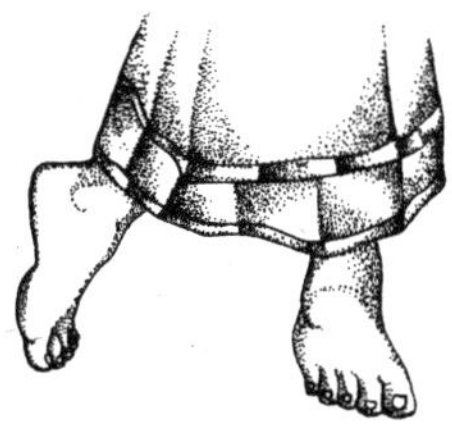

Śiva's dance composed of *karaṇas, aṅgahāras* and *piṇḍībandhas* inspired Pārvatī for a *sukumāra prayoga*. The performance was seen by the *gaṇas* (attendants of Śiva). The chief among them, Nandī and Bhadra, witnessed the formation of *piṇḍīs*, which were symbolical formations of the *āyudhas* (weapons), *varṇas* (the *akṣara*/letter associated with the deity) or the *patākās* (flags which carry the emblem) of the *devatās*. The *piṇḍīs* were named according to the *lakṣaṇas* (quality) of the particular deity. *Nāṭya-Śāstra* also states that the *piṇḍībandhas* are group dances, and may be performed by one, two, three or four dancers. When it is performed by one dancer, it is called *piṇḍī*, two dancers together, i.e., two *piṇḍīs* together is called *śṛṅkhalika* (a cluster like formation), three dancers together create the *latābandha piṇḍī* (a net like formation) and four dancers together with the help of the *piṇḍī, śṛṅkhalika*, and *latābandha*, create the *bhedayaka piṇḍī-bandha*. *Nāṭya-Śāstra* also states that the *piṇḍīs* are formed for many reasons, but it is important for the actor/dancer to pay attention to the *yoni* (the origin), *yantra* (formation of ritualistic diagram), *bhadrāsana* (*uttama āsana*, i.e., selection of the right *bhūmi*/place and *āsana*), and *śikṣāyoga* (which is the practise of *nṛtta* embellished with *karaṇa, aṅgahāras*, in a manner which makes it a *sādhanā*/*yoga*). We thus have a very specific reference to the cordoning of space through the use of *recakas, aṅgahāras* and *piṇḍī-bandhas* (which includes *gati, cāri, sthānaka* as well) by the dancer, whose ultimate purpose is to please the deity/deities by creating a semblance of their *āyudhas, vāhanas*, emblems or even deeds

→ to inner sound (*śabda*), the subtle body, to *mantra, yantra* and to *āsana* (body posture). A body has *yantra* (form) by the nature of its posture, *āsana*. It has *mantra* by the nature of its breathing (*prāṇāyāma*). He further elaborates "The body is the laboratory for *sādhanā*. It should be healthy. The subtle *vyāna-prāṇa* associated with the element ether, is directly connected with the *yantra* of the body (i.e., its posture). Thus, in order to control the *vyāna*, posture, must also be controlled. Inner sound (*śabda*) and posture (*āsana*) are interdependent. All *sādhanās* make use of *āsana*, it being the "base" free from strain and cosmically in tune for the process of inner awakening."

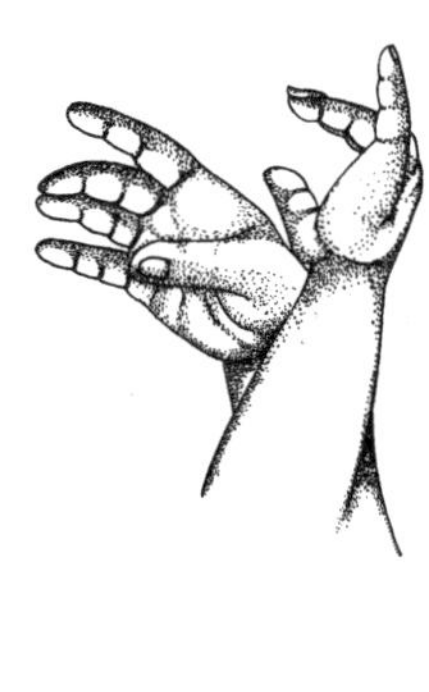

(represented symbolically, e.g., in the *Gaṅgāvataraṇa karaṇa*, the symbol of *dhārā*, also reminds the story of Śiva holding the Gaṅgā in his locks, when she falls from the heaven with a force which could have pushed the Earth into the *pātāla*. Similarly, we have the *nāgasarpita karaṇa* which pleases the Devī, the *niśumbhita karaṇa* which satisfies Śiva. The *Abhinavabhāratī* states that the *mayūra, lalita* and other *karaṇa*s together create the *Śivapiṇḍī*, just as the *viṣṇukrānta* (100) and the *cakramaṇḍala* (53) *karaṇa* indicate actions related to Viṣṇu) with the ultimate aim to receive their blessings.[31] Though the *Nāṭya-Śāstra* states that *nṛtta* is only performed for embellishment and auspiciousness and has no meaning, yet Bharata says that it is performed to overcome the shortcomings of *gāyana, vādana* and *abhinaya* (singing, playing instruments and acting), just as song is sung to disguise the shortcomings in *abhinaya*, and *vādana* is used to disguise the shortcomings in singing).[32] This statement is very suggestive and becomes more meaningful and more vibrant if we consider *nṛtta* as *vyañjanā* or suggestion, for it is only for the love of the art that Śiva, the formless, who pervades the entire universe, chooses to assume a form to enjoy his own cosmic dance !

31. *Nāṭya-Śāstra*, with commentaries *Abhinavabhāratī, Madhusūdanī* and *Bālakrīḍā*, infra. See Ch. 4 for more descriptions and details *NŚ*, 4.264, p. 406; Śiva dances with *karaṇa, aṅgahāra*s, *piṇḍī-bandha*s and teaches the art to Taṇḍu; *NŚ*, 4.256, p. 396, Pārvatī is inspired and performs *sukumāra prayoga*; *NŚ*, 4.257, p. 397, Nandī and Bhadra witness the formation of *piṇḍa*s in the dance; *NŚ*, 4.263, p. 404, states *piṇḍī*s should be named according to the emblem or symbol sign of the deity. *Piṇḍī* means *āyudha*s, *varaṇa*s, flags, emblems, etc., of deities, see commentary, p. 397. It also states that the *piṇḍī-bandha*s were named *salakṣaṇa*, i.e., the names were meaningful. *NŚ*, 4.292-294, pp. 462-63, explains the four kinds of *piṇḍī* formations. *NŚ*, 4.295, p. 464, states the reasons for *piṇḍī* formations. Also see commentary of Abhinava Gupta, *Abhinavabhāratī* and of *Bālakrīḍā*, p. 405, for *gaṅgāvataraṇa, nāgasarpita, viṣṇukrānta karaṇa*s. Also see *NŚ*, 4.259-264, pp. 399-406, for details of *piṇḍī*s.

32. *Ibid.*, *Nāṭya-Śāstra*, 4.268-269, pp. 419-29.

We thus see that the *Nāṭya-Śāstra*, through the enumeration of *karaṇas*, *aṅgahāras*, *sthānakas*, *maṇḍalas*, *cāris*, *piṇḍī-bandhas*, *tāla*, *laya*, *abhinaya*, the building of the *raṅgamañca*, aspects of *nṛtta*, fully reveals the awareness of the concepts of time and space, the art of arrangement, on the linear as well as horizontal/vertical levels and the extension of space beyond parameters and raises the art of dancing to a level where it becomes a vehicle for the ultimate deliverance, when it becomes the embodiment of *rasa*. The lines and formations created in solo or group dances/performances are actually creation of *yantras* by the dancers. These movements/ formations are today popularly referred to as choreography in dance.[33] That choreography is inherent in any group/solo performance of dance, may be seen in the very ancient system of our folk dances, where the dancers move clock-wise, anti-clockwise, in circles, squares, triangles, diagonals, lines, etc., in perfect unison to the accompanying music and rhythm (*fig.* 1).

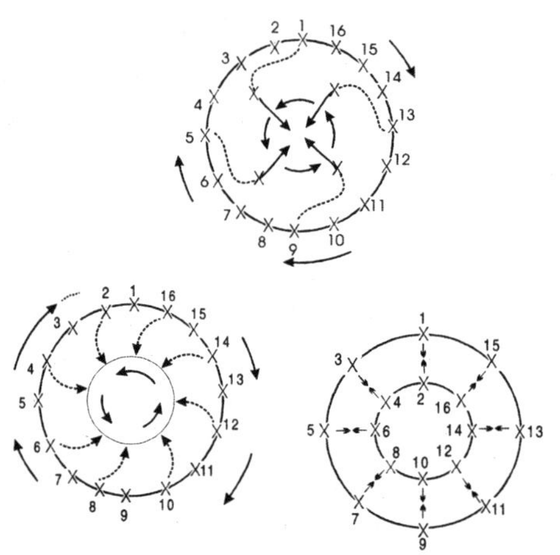

Fig. 1 Movement of dancers on folk songs.

33. *Kala*, Journal of Indian Art History Congress, vol. VI, 1999-2000, ed. M.N. Tiwari, K. Giri, in which is published Choreography : A Quest in India's Cultural Heritage by R. Srivastva. Choreography shows the impact of the west in word alone. Though the formations are ancient and traditional yet the understanding has shifted from the religious/metaphysical to the secular, mundane.

The choreographic notion played a significant role in dance sequences even in stone or in colour (*Pls.* 32 & 33).[34]

The art of *Kathaka* dance is the product of human organization and cultural enterprise and it has thus acquired some enduring value (artistic, social, philosophical and spiritual) which have been transmitted from generation to generation in the *guru-śiṣya paramparā*, in the process of adoption and adaptation. The continuity is however, maintained through a repeated pattern in a spatial and temporal frame, channellized through the various modes of transmission : imitation, practise, meditation and creation. Dance if performed as a ritual not only sustains the continuity of a very ancient art form but also uplifts both the art and the artist much above the mundane level of everyday experiences. The art then becomes instrumental to, or a medium to unravel the secrets of nature, to understand the cosmic relationships through opening the doors and windows for inner experiences. This is the stage when the artist becomes a *sādhaka,* the art his *sādhanā,* the entire macrocosm gets engulfed, or manifested in the microcosm, the cycle of "wholeness" gets completed. This is the truth, the essence of *Kathaka,* as a dance form, from man to divinity; the art and science of the *yantra,* when artistic creations become magical diagrams ! This is a step towards a more deeper and a more philosophical understanding to see how through the use of various symbols, *mudrās*, *sthānakas*/*āsanas*, *Kathaka* makes an effort to understand and translate the Ultimate Reality, because in dance there is very definitely a pervasive tendency to dramatize the cosmogony by creating on *bhūmi* (earth) a reduced version of the cosmos, both in the movements of the dancer in space as well as the lines and diagrams which he creates on the earth (the dancing floor) through the skillful movements of his feet.

---

34. *Kala*, Journal of Indian Art History Congress, vol. VI, 1999-2000, For more detailed discussion.

Samapāda, Samabhaṅga and Samadaṁśa

The very first stance in *Kathaka* is, the dancer standing in *samapāda, samabhaṅga* with a *samadaṁśa-mudrā* in the hands (see *Fig.* 2 & *Pl.* 14). When the feet are placed naturally on the ground with a distance of one *tāla* or eight *aṅgula*s between them it is *samapāda* (see *Fig.* 3 & *Pl.* 15). Its presiding deity is Brahmā, the benedictory blessings should be received in this *sthāna* (position).[35] *Samabhaṅga* denotes the equipoised body where the *sūtra* or the plumb line passes through the navel from the crown of the head to a point midway between the heels. There is complete symmetry between the left and the right sides of the body. When the forefinger touches (*samadasta*) the thumb, and the palm is, *ābhugnanata* (slightly curved), it is called *samadaṁśa hasta*, one of its uses mentioned in the *Nāṭya-*

Fig. 2

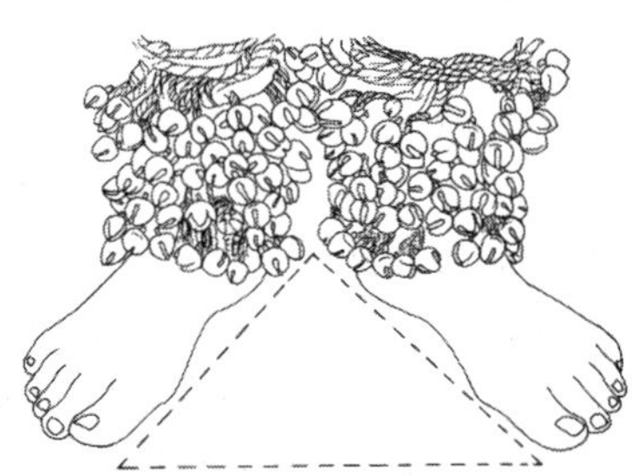

Fig. 3

35. *Nāṭya-Śāstra*, 10.58-59; infra, p. 996. Also see *Abhinaya Darpaṇa*, v. 275, p. 88, tr. Puru Dadicha, Bindu Prakashan, Ujjain, 1988. Also see *Saṅgītaratnākara*, vol. IV, 1041.3, p. 92 and IV. 7.315, p. 160, ed., S. Subrahamanyam Sastri, The Adyar Library and Research Centre, Madras, 1953.

Śāstra is in the practise of concentration in *yoga*.[36]

The author however, feels that the constant use of this *mudrā* in *Kathaka* dance points to its association with the *vyākhyāna-mudrā* in the *śilpa* texts, and the *prabodha-mudrā* (*cin-mudrā*) as described by saints. The right hand of Śiva's Dakṣiṇāmūrti is in the *cin-mudrā*. According to Sivaramamurti, "it is in the attitude of enlightenment (the thumb and the pointing finger brought together) as suggestive of the immanence of the almighty in the individual, the universal self witnessed in the orb of the sun : *sa yas cayam puruṣa yas chāsāvāditye sa ekaḥ* — *Taittirīya Upaniṣad* (3.10.4)."[37] To be especially marked is that both the hands in *samadaṁśa* is a further stress on *yoga*, *dhyāna* and the negligible nature of the finite *alpa* before the infinite *bhūmi*.[38] The *dharmacakra-mudrā* of Buddha is in the *saṁyukta hasta-mudrā* of *samadaṁśa hasta* and is an indicator to transcendence, *yoga*, meditation or *dhyāna*, and infinitesimal *stoka*[39] Also as Medhā-Dakṣiṇāmūrti or Jñāna-Dakṣiṇāmūrti, the right hand of Śiva is in *cin-mudrā*. In several sculptures of Naṭarāja the hand in *abhaya* is shown in *samadaṁśa*/*cin-mudrā*. According to Sivaramamurti, "Śiva Naṭarāja with *samadaṁśa* suggests his teaching the art particularly *lāsya*."[40] He also says "Though *samadaṁśa* is a *hasta* for gathering flowers and Ratnakara used it in this sense,

---

36. *Nāṭya-Śāstra*, 9.110-116, *op. cit.*, p. 913-14, The *Abhinaya Darpaṇa*, vs 154-156, infra, p. 49 calls this *hasta haṁsāsya*. *Saṅgītaratnākara*, 7.122-127, infra, calls it *arala*. One of its uses stated is that when placed against the heart of men it is applicable in benediction and it should be moved clockwise for the circumambulation of deities. The *Abhinaya Darpaṇa* states one of its use as *upadeśa*.

37. C. Sivaramamurti, *Dakshinamurti Glory of Learning*, Lecture delivered at BHU, Varanasi under Madan Mohan Malviya Memorial Lecture on 22nd and 23rd July 1981, manuscript yet to be published.

38. *Nāṭya-Śāstra*, 9.114; infra, pp. 914-15.

39. C. Sivaramamurti, *Dakshinamurti Glory of Learning*, *op. cit.*

40. *Ibid.*

Bharata took it to mean teaching or imparting of knowledge, *jñāna-mudrā* and gentle dance, *lāsya nartana* apart from the attitude of worship, *arcanā*, where the pointing finger moves away frequently from the thumb, but here in the case of Śiva it signifies not only the *vyākhyāna-mudrā* but also the *mokṣa* or bliss or coming together of the *jīvātmā* or *paramātmā*."[41] In other words, the *vyākhyāna-mudrā* (or *samadaṁśa* or *cin-mudrā*) symbolizes the *prabodha* or understanding to distinguish reality from illusion. The explanatory attitude of this *mudrā*, in which the forefingers are brought together with the thumb, thus suggests *prabodha* in which the *jīvātmā* and the *paramātmā* (individual soul and the universal soul) come together. In Tāntric terminology we could say, it is only a method of realizing/experiencing or building a strong relation between the human essence, microcosm and the divine macrocosm (*Pl.* 14 & *fig.* 2).

With the two arms turned from the elbow towards the body, a little lower from the level of the chest, closer towards the navel, we can very clearly see the creation of two distinct triangles. The triangle in tāntric symbolism is a representation of the divinity, the source of existence, "conceived as the principle of speech (*Śabda-Brahman*) or the word principle (*vāc-tattva*)."[42]

The navel as the centre of the body symbolizes the *bindu*

41. C. Sivaramamurti, *Dakshinamurti Glory of Learning*, *op. cit.*

42. Ajit Mukherji, *Tantra Art Its Philosophy and Physics*, infra, p. 17, wherein he also says that the three lower stages of manifestation, corresponding to the *icchā-śakti* (the power of will), *jñāna-śakti* (the power of knowledge) and *kriyā-śakti* (the power of action), also spoken of as intention, formulation and expression are symbolized as the three sides of the triangle. Also see *Saṅgītaratnākara*, vol. I, tr. R.K. Shringy, Prem Lata Sharma, IGNCA Munshiram Manoharlal Delhi, 1999, p. 87, where it is said that, according to *Ṣaṭacakranirūpaṇa*, the foundational cycle is the place where the female principle represented by a triangle, the *yoni* known as *traipura* is located, and in the triangle is set the male principle represented by the *svayambhū* (self born) *liṅga*.

which contains the two poles within itself (zero and infinity) and all that lies in between. It also symbolizes the ultimate point of power beyond which a thing or energy cannot be further contracted or condensed. It is both the nucleus of matter (*jara*) as well as the nucleus of radiant consciousness (*caitanya*).[43] In dance also, the navel occupies the central position. Though the *Nāṭya-Śāstra* does not explicitly deal with the *nābhi*, yet it is founded on the Āyurvedic and yogic concept of the navel as the centre of body movement, and as the seat of energy.[44] The *Saṅgītaratnākara* describes the *nābhi* in detail and calls it *brahma-granthī*.[45]

As a student when the author was learning dance from her *guru*, Sri Vikram Singh, she was often told by her *guru* to let the movements grow out of the body, which she could not understand at that time. Today after so many years, the truth seems to have been revealed : with the feet in *samapāda*, the torso in *samabhaṅga* and the *samadaṁśa-mudrā* in the hands, the body reaches a poise and balance as the *rekhā* (the spinal chord, straight line) holds the body in an equipoise, a yogic posture. This may also explain the fact why *Kathaka* lacks the rigidity of the other dances. The same composition is danced in a number of ways by different dancers or even by one dancer himself. With the formation of this *yantra* the dancer enters into a state of *dhyāna*, which gives birth to *jñāna* or knowledge which is then expressed through movements and *abhinaya*[46] (*Pls.* 14-15 & *figs*. 2-3).

43. *Ibid.*, pp. 28-30.

44. *Kalātattavakośa*, vol. II, *op. cit.*, p. 43.

45. *Saṅgītaratnākara*, 1.1.3-4, *op. cit.*, p. 111. Also see *Kalātattavakośa*, vol. II, infra, p. 43., vol. II, *op. cit.*, p. 43.

46. In the flanking figures of Viṣṇu sculptures, one arm is bent from the elbow to the navel, a little higher/lower, while the other arms falls loosely on the thigh, a stance very clearly visible in the *thāṭa* section of *Kathaka* even today. For a more detailed description see *Kathaka : Its origin and development : A study based on Ancient and Medieval Sculptures and Paintings*, by the author (unpublished).

After taking this stance the body of the *Kathaka* dancer (in a traditional *Kathaka* performance) starts to sway gently, to the rhythmic sound produced from the instruments accompanying the dancer. This is done through a very controlled breathing by the dancer. In the yogic or tāntric terminology this is the *prāṇāyāma*. The movement is very subtle in the manner of the flame of the burning wick of an oil lamp. The symbolism is that through the breath, the fire inside the body is activated. The *Kulārṇava Tantra* states : "As the body is to the *jīva*, as oil is to the lamp, so is *yantra*, the established seat of all the Deities."[47] A fourth century AD *Bodhisattva* image from Bodh-Gayā evinces a being whose essence is enlightenment. The image as such appears engrossed in a deep trance controlling his breath like a *yogī* and this strictly disciplined figure conceived within an isosceles triangle calls for a comparison with flickerless flame of a lamp (*nivāta niṣkrampa iva pradīpam*).

Tā-Thei-Tata

The three basic *bols* or mnemonic syllables on which the entire edifice of *Kathaka* dance is built. The various combinations of these primary *bols* results in the production of beautiful, simple and complex sound patterns, both in the *tatkāra* (footwork) and *nṛtta* (pure dance) section of *Kathaka*. The author feels that the three mnemonic syllables may justly be called the *bījākṣaras* and may be found in the proverbial three steps of Viṣṇu which he took in traversing the earth and the terrestrial spaces : Viṣṇu as Trivikrama, (see *Pl.* 4 & 5) in which he begins in the *samapāda* and the three steps measuring *ākāśa*, *pātāla* and the *bhūloka*, falling on three different elements, air, water and earth, creating three different sounds are the *bījas* for the dance.

The author was repeatedly told about the great importance and the mystical significance of these *bols* by her *guru*. She

47. Nik Douglas, *Tantra, Yoga*, p. 65, *op. cit.*

was told that if she could master these *bol*s she could conquer the universe. Unable to understand at the time, the *rahasya* (mystery) is now revealed to her.[48] It is reported that Bindadin, the great doyen of *Kathaka*, practised *tatkāra* for nine years !

In *tatkāra*, the position of the feet is in *samapāda*, but the movements of the feet create different *yantra*s (geometrical diagrams) on the ground below. In the *Nāṭya- Śāstra* there is a reference to *stobha-kriyā*s, which in the translation reads that the foot movements during the *pūjā* should be made to accompany the playing of drums and there should be no song sung then, but only meaningless syllables chanted. These mnemonic syllables are referred to as *paṭākṣaras,* and the word which comes closest to it is *vāckaraṇa*, which are used both in songs and in drums and reveal association with the *vīṇā*.[49] *Saṅgītaratnākara* mentions six kinds of *ghuṅghrū* (bells) sounds. The *prayoga*s mentioned in this thirteenth-century treatise on

48. R. Srivastava, *Kathaka : Its origin and development : A Study based on Ancient and Medieval Sculptures and Paintings,* unpublished, infra, for a more detailed discussion. The author has traced the origin of *Kathaka* to Viṣṇu, who is related to *ākāśa* (*V. Pur.*, 1.14.32), the conch in his hand symbolizes *kha* (space), (*V. Dhar. Pur.*, III.85.17) and as we have seen *ākāśa* is thought to be the material medium of sound. S.R. 1.2.57, maintains that the body obtains sound, the faculty of hearing from space.

49. *Nāṭya-Śāstra*, vol. I, Chs. i-xxvii, ed., Manamohan Ghosh, 2nd edn., Granthalaya Pvt. Ltd., Calcutta, 1967, see. Ch. v., 103-104, also see Kumbhā Mahārānā, *Saṅgītarāja*, vol. I, ed. Prem Lata Sharma, Hindu Vishvavidyalaya Sanskrit Pub. Board, Varanasi. 1963, p. 110, wherein it is explained that *pāṭhya* is not external to *saṅgīta*, as it is fundamentally concerned with *nāda*. In fact, it is the manifestation of *nāda*. "As for the presence or absence of suggestible meanings in sound (syllabic or non-syllabic) it may be said that there is no essential difference between the two, as both are equally powerful in their suggestive power (*Vyañjana-Śakti*). The difference lies only in the presence of primary meaning (*Abhidhā-Śakti*) in syllabic sounds and the absence of that in non-syllable ones. This means that syllabic sounds are more meaningful than non-syllabic sounds."

music and dance are even today in vogue in the present performing tradition of *Kathaka* :

1. *Padivata* : the up and down (*kuṭṭana*) movement on the ground of both the heels, with the forepart held to the ground. This very clearly creates two distinct centres (*bindus*).

2. *Apaḍapa* : Striking the ground with the sole, in an up and down movement.

3. *Siripata* : Sliding the foot forward and backward repeatedly with the sole holding the ground. This creates distinct lines on the floor (earth).

4. *Alagapāta* : Shaking both the feet gently in the air alternatively.

5. *Sirihira* : Keeping one foot in the *sama* position, the other foot is pushed forward and its shank shaken. The shanks may also be shaken by keeping both the feet naturally on the ground.

6. *Khaluhula* : The up and down movement on the ground with the heel of the left foot and its forepart touching the ground and the circular movement to the left and right of the other feet with its forepart touching the ground.

All these movements create distinct line formations. According to Prem Lata Sharma, all these names are *deśī* and in fact suggestive of the sound in their production, besides this, these non-sensible syllables also help the audience to concentrate more on the rhythm, because there is no distraction by way of comprehending the meaning of the text. Needless to repeat, that the movements of the feet create distinct *rekhās*, *maṇḍalas*, triangles on the ground below. The *bhūmi* in this case becomes a *yantra*, which gets empowered with the *mantra*, the sound of the meaningless mnemonic syllables created by

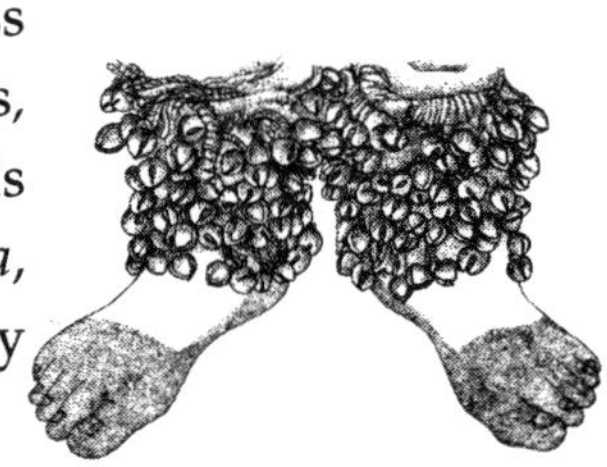

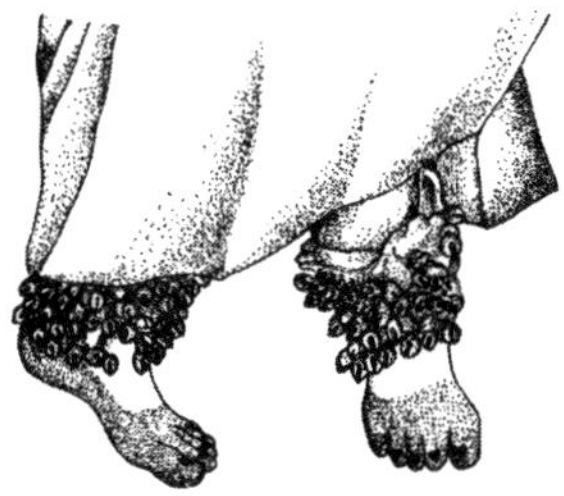

the striking movements of the feet[50] (see *Pl.* 19-21).

It would be pertinent to mention here that in the oral tradition of *Kathaka* we have heard of dancers performing a *ṭukaḍā* (composition) and creating the figure of an elephant on the floor. Both Bindadin Maharaja and Achchan Maharaja created such *yantras*. Even Sunder Prasad Ji, the doyen of the Jaipur Gharānā wanted to teach the author, but unfortunately it could not materialize.

Cakkara (Pirouette)

Kathaka is well known for its *cakkaras* or pirouettes, which are executed with great skill, speed and dexterity. Keeping the plumb line straight, the dancer spins round on his heels/toes raising the other foot above the ground. He may take a single or a hundred and two hundred *cakkaras*. The arms are spread out at the starting of the *cakkara* and brought back to the starting position (both the arms bent from the elbow towards the chest, a little lower, towards the navel, the palms facing down, holding a *samadaṁśa-mudrā*) after the completion of each *cakkara* (see *Pl.* 22).

The *cakkaras* are only a transference of the *maṇḍala* which in the *Tantra-Śāstra* signifies the twin acts of emanation and absorption[51] (see *Pl.* 23). The *maṇḍala* is a natural extension of the central point (*bindu*). It is the whole universe in itself, it is a "cosmogram." The ideology of the *maṇḍala* allows the aspirant/devotee to symbolically enter into the *maṇḍala* and partake of the powers that reside within. It is ultimately to bring harmony and balance. Kṛṣṇa performs the *rāsa* with the *gopīs* in a *maṇḍalakāra* formation. The *cakra* (disc) of Viṣṇu

50. *Saṅgītaratnākara*, vol. IV, 7.1303-1313, infra, pp. 385-88, ed. Subrāhmaṇya Sastri, also see tr. Kunjunni Raja and Radha Bernier, pp. 195-96.

51. S.K. Rao Ramachandra, *Tantras, op. cit.*, pp. 14-17, he says "if the centre point is the unmanifest power (*avyakta*) the *maṇḍala* is the manifest counterpart (*vyakta*)".

identifies with the design of the *maṇḍala*. Coomaraswamy says,

> certain of the Kṛṣṇa mysteries such as the Rāsa Maṇḍala may have a very remote ancestry, perhaps an esoteric Vaiṣṇava tradition remained more or less secret until the *Bhāgavata Purāṇa* and the subsequent mediaeval Sanskrit and Hindi literature of devotion, it became a leading theme of religious art.[52]

In the *Mahābhārata*, Viṣṇu says that he is gratified by the worship of brāhmaṇas, and those who make offering in a circle.[53] Also the *cakra maṇḍala*, 56th *karaṇa* and *Viśvakrānta*, 100th *karaṇa* are used to show actions related to Viṣṇu.[54] According to Boner, the *yantra*s and the *mantra*s are abstract geometrical symbols of the same metaphysical conceptions and are formed on similar concentric figurations, she says that the concentric organization of all manner of sacred symbolic representation seems to be an inescapable necessity,

> The circle is always the fundamental determining factor. Between the centre and the circumference of the circle there is an indissoluble connection of polarity, from which nothing can escape. The movements thrown out by the centre are collected by the circumference and reversed towards the centre or an unending movement may arise and flow round the circumference held together by the centre.[55]

---

52. A. Coomaraswamy, *Rajput Painting*, vol. I, text, pp. 28-29, Motilal Banarsidass, Varanasi, 1976.
53. *Mahābhārata*, XIII. 26, Anuśāsan Parva, Pt. II, vol. 17, ed. R.N. Dandekar, Bhandarkar Oriental Research Institute, Poona, 1966, p. 666.
54. *Nāṭya-Śāstra*, ed. Madhusudan Sastri, infra, p. 406; also see *NŚ* 3.21-23, p. 207, for references to *maṇḍala*s on the *raṅga* (stage) and the centre of the *raṅga* for the consecration of Brahmā seated on the *padma*. See commentary, *Bālakrīḍā*.
55. Alice Boner, *Principles of Composition*, infra, pp. 24-25; also see Preface.

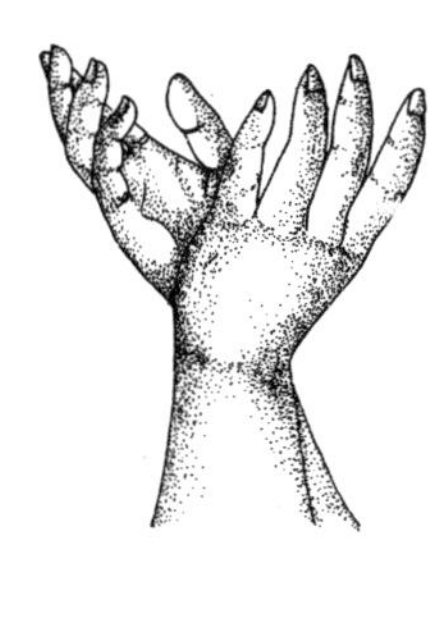

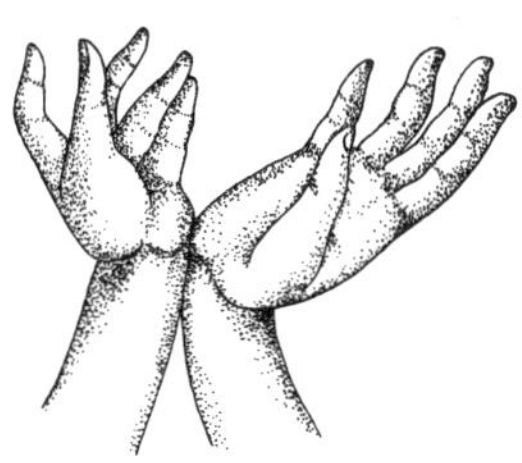

Both in the *Yoga-Śāstra* and the *Tantra-Śāstra* there are references to different *cakra*s situated in the different parts of the body. They are shown in the lotus formation, e.g., the *ādhāra cakra*, between the anus and the genitals is a four-pettalled lotus; the *svādhiṣṭhāna-cakra* at the root of the genitals is six-petalled lotus; the *maṇipūraka cakra* situated around the navel is a ten petalled lotus; the *anāhata cakra* situated in the heart is a twelve-petalled lotus, the *viśuddhi cakra* situated in the throat-larynx is a sixteen-petalled lotus; the *lalanā cakra* situated in the back of the neck has twelve petals, the *ājñā cakra* is located between the eye-brows and is a three-petalled lotus, *mānas cakra* situated in the mind has six petals; the *sahasrapatra cakra* is located in the cerebral aperture and is a thousand-petalled lotus. The *Saṅgītaratnākara* (1.2.140-141, p. 96, 97), states that meditation of the eight, eleventh and twelfth petals of the *anāhata cakra* gives proficiency in music, while concentration on the fourth, sixth and tenth petals destroys ones capacity for music. With reference to the *sahasrapatra-kamala* in the *brahmarandhra*, the *Saṅgītarāja* also states that the accomplishment (*siddhi*) of *Gītā* and the like is attained by one who is inundated with the nectar (*amṛta*) flowing from the *kamala* (or *soma cakra*). Thus, according to Kumbhā, the real accomplishment of *Gītā* can be attained only through accomplishment in *yoga* which is symbolized by *somapāna* from the *brahmarandhra*.[56]

In *Kathaka* dance, the *cakra/maṇḍala* is created both on the *bhūmi* (dancing floor) by the movements of the feet of the dancer as well as in the space around by the opened

56. *Saṅgītaratnākara*, vol. I,1.2.120-141, tr. R.K. Shringey, Prem Lata Sharma, infra, pp. 84-97. Note : The *soma cakra*, not included in the scheme of the main psychophysical centres, has not been mentioned here. It is mentioned on p. 94, S.R., Same edition. Also see Kumbhā, Mahārāṇa, *Saṅgītarāja, op. cit.*, p. 111.

arms of the dancer. The circle as suggestive of *purṇatā* or completeness, also eradicates the concept of fragments.

Trām

A gesture which is usually used in the performance of the *bol trām*, in which the dancer takes a small jump and with both the arms raised above the level of the head in the front, the hands in *kuñcita patākā* making a gesture encircling, circumambulating each other, touching at the wrist is not merely a *nṛtta* movement. It is much more symbolical and suggestive. The movement is used to show the lotus flower (see *Pls.* 24-27). The lotus has been associated with the Hindu thought and tradition since ancient times. The creator Brahmā is always shown seated on a lotus, which stems out of the navel of Viṣṇu, identified by scholars as a combination of the aspects of Vāsudeva, Kṛṣṇa, Nārāyaṇa.[57] The goddess Lakṣmī, rose out from the ocean at the time of *amṛta-manthana*, she was sweated on a lotus. One of the appellants of Viṣṇu is *padmanābha*. Coomaraswamy states that

> . . . there are also frequent representations of Viṣṇu alone or with Lakṣmī enthroned upon a lotus seat (*padmāsana*) or of Devī similarly represented. These figures are often surrounded by worshipping figures. They correspond to the *dhyāna mantram* which are visually realized in personal worship of the *iṣṭa devatā*.[58]

Sivaramamurti states that the lotus may be taken to be suggestive of the water form of Śiva.[59] The lotus as a symbol,

57. Prem Lata Sharma, *Indian Aesthetics and Musicology : The Art and Science of Indian Music*, ed. U. Sharma Amnaya Prakasana, Varanasi, 2000, see pp. 14, 15, 20, 21.

58. A. Coomaraswamy, *Rajput Painting*, vol. I, infra, p. 40.

59. C. Sivaramamurti, *Naṭarāja In Art Thought And Literature*, Publications Division, Ministry of Information and Broadcasting, New Delhi, 1994 (Reprint), p. 357.

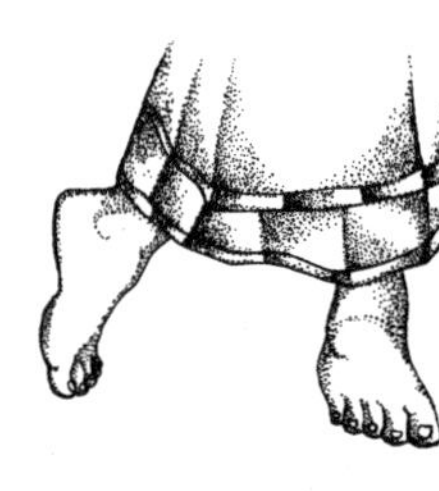

thus caters to the three worlds: this world, the world below and the world above, corresponding to the elements: earth, water and light. In fact, it embraces all the elements and forms of the world. Its openings and closings are a measure of time : day and night. In *Kathaka*, the gesture however creates a circle in the space above the head, though it may be taken in other places also, as near the heart. The symbolism of the circle has already been discussed.

Puṣpapuṭa Hasta

When two *sarpaśīrṣa hasta*s are joined, they form a *puṣpapuṭa hasta*. Its uses include, accepting fruits or water, evening worship, imbibing *mantra*s, etc.[60] This is a very largely used *hasta* in *Kathaka* especially when the dancer takes the stance

Fig. 4

60. *Abhinaya Darpaṇa*, vs. 182-83, p. 59, tr. Puru Dadica, Bindu Prakashan, Ujjain, 1968, p. 59. Also see *Saṅgītaratnākara* 7. 196-97, ed., S. Subrāhmaṇya Sastri, infra, p. 54.

in which the legs are crossed in *svastika*, the body is in *samabhaṅga* and the two arms after enacting the *puṣpapuṭa* at the side spread out, the right generally going up in a *samadaṁśa-mudrā* facing out and the left going forward a little to the side, with a *samadaṁśa* facing down. Both the arms having a slight curve. It may also be enacted vice-versa. The symbolism in the movement is the humble begging or acceptance of *jñāna* and the dissemination of that *jñāna* or knowledge. The *svastika* of the feet denotes the auspiciousness of that knowledge (see *Pl.* 28, 29, *fig.* 4 & 5).

Svastika

A very common stance taken in *Kathaka*, in the standing posture. While one leg is in *samapāda*, the other crosses it from the back or front, resting on the toes like a *sucī* (see *Pl.* 29, *fig.* 5). It is commonly seen in the figures of Kr̥ṣṇa in the

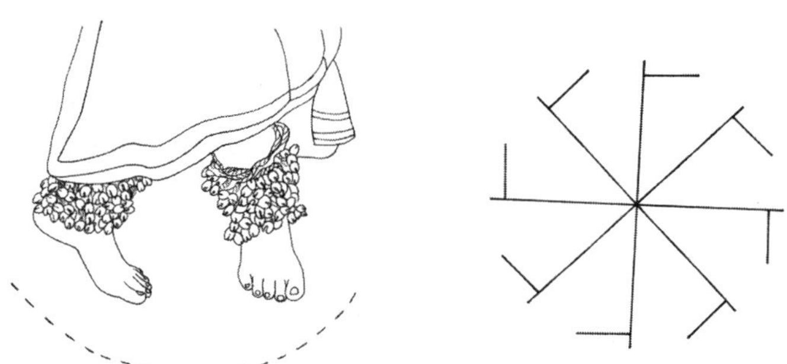

Fig. 5

tribhaṅgī. The *Saṅgītaratnākara* calls this *puruṣthottānatala* and deals it under *deśī* postures.[61] The *svastika* as a symbol shows allegiance with the sun, the symbol of celestial fire and is thus equated with the sun. It is also considered to be a symbolic form of disc, wheel, lotus and prosperity. It is

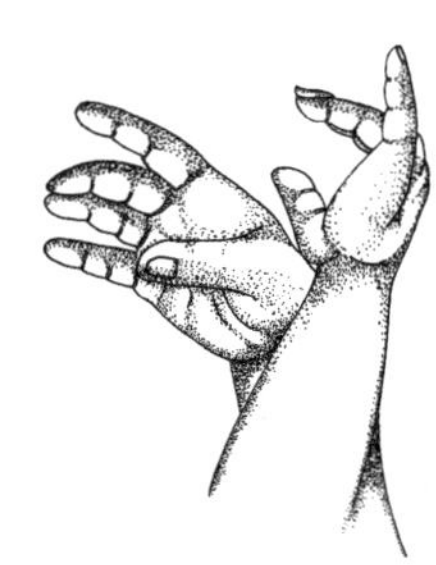

61. *Saṅgītaratnākara*, 7.1079, p. 331, and 7.318, p. 93. Also see *Abhinaya Darpaṇa*, v. 269, tr. Puru Dadich, infra, p. 86. Also see *Nāṭya-Śāstra*: 10.34, ed. Madhusudan Sastri, infra, pp. 977-88.

interesting to note that Viṣṇu in the *Ṛgveda* is considered an aspect of the Sun god.[62]

The *svastika*, thus, a symbol of the sun and the *cakra* represents the principle of life and movement "that transfers the dwarf into a giant or the microcosm into the macrocosm, or again the centre into the diameter or vice-versa. It is called *Ṛkvan*, that is the rhythmical movements. Owing to the efficacy of this movement a perfect circle is evolved at each and every point on the two sides of the centre enclosing within its womb a *svastika* of four right angles of 360°."[63] Even the surface of the earth, in traditional Indian cosmology is demarcated by the north-south-east-west points. It is for this reason that it is represented by ideogram or *maṇḍala* of a square. The earth is therefore, called *caturbhṛṣti* (four-cornered) and is symbolically shown as the *pṛthvī-maṇḍala*, though in itself its shape is circular (see *Pl.* 29, *fig.* 5).

The Varada Hasta

A stance in which the left hand is bent from the elbow and brought in line with the chest, towards the navel with a *samadaṁśa hasta* palm facing down. Fingers slightly rounded, while the right hand is lowered down with a *varada hasta*, the fingers pointing down and palm facing up. The feet may be in *samapāda* or in the *svastika*, with the weight slightly more on the left. In *Kathaka*, the forceful opening out of the hands with the stress on the fingers in taking this stance, frequently at the end of a *bandiśa*, brings a dazzle to the performance, though the stance brings to the mind a ritualistic association : the pouring of water, or

62. B.C. Sinha, *Hinduism and Symbol Worship*, Agam Kala Prakashan Delhi, 1983, pp. 76-84.

63. Padma Sudhi, *Symbols of Art Religion and Philosophy*, p. 41, Intellectual Publishing House, New Delhi, 1988.

offering of flowers at the time of *pūjā* or *yajñas*, which are performed for fulfilment or achievement of desires and goals. Its use in *Kathaka*, where the dancer takes this stance symbolizes the ritualistic/religious aspect of the dance. The dancer completes the composition in this stance as if it is a *yajña* completed (see *Pl.* 30, *fig.* 6).

Fig. 6

Ghaṭa (Pitcher)

The *gagarī gata*s are distinctly unique to *Kathaka* (see *Pl.* 31). Though mimetic in character, they are performed to the accompaniment of instrumental music. They draw their inspiration from the narrative hymns of the Vedas which were accompanied with ritualistic ceremonies and music and dance. These *gata*s show a clear impact or association with the ceremony of the *mahāvrata*, in which maids and slave girls, with water jars or pots on their heads dance round the *marjali*, singing popular songs and beating, the ground with their feet. The *pūrṇa kumbha* or full vase is pre-eminently a Vedic motif. The *amṛta-kalaśa* placed on the pinnacle of the *garbha-gṛha*, symbolizes the vessel of deathlessness. In the Indian ritualistic culutre, all ritual

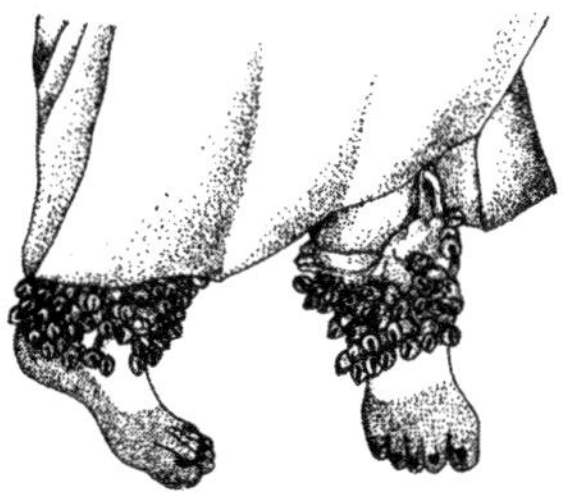

worship starts with the establishment of the *ghaṭa,* the ceremonial jar, placed in front of the deity's image or pedestal. When the deity is invoked through *mantra*s and is invited to descend into the sacred water contained in the vessel — *ghaṭa,* it becomes charged and thus becomes a powerful means of contact between the *sādhaka* (devotee) and the cosmos. The jar also becomes vibrant by being ritually established on a lump of clay, rice or *maṇḍala* diagram.

We may, thus, safely conclude that the principles of composition in the art form — *Kathaka* dance, are studied and laboured, because in India the evolution of the arts, whether painting, sculpture or dance, has been the work of successive generations and the traditional artists were dedicated to the realization of metaphysical/religious ideas. It is for this reason that the vigour of conception and its execution is enhanced by a powerful substratum of transcendent thought. The traditional artists, it appears, were in a profound communion with Nature, because they were fully aware of the significance of movements, their origin, manifestation and expression, the lines, the dots, the circles, triangles and squares, their sensuousness as well as their delicate inflections, their feelings and *bhāva*s. As Boner aptly says :

> the traditional artist was dedicated to the realisation of a metaphysical or religious idea and not the realization of his own personality. The rules according to which he worked were not arbitrary or conventional, but were derived from spiritual conceptions which were broad and comprehensive enough to allow him to work in the fire and freedom of his own inner vision. Where everything grows out of and is controlled by the same principle, there is no difference between law and freedom.[64]

---

64. Alice Boner, *Principles of Composition in Hindu Sculpture,* infra, p. 36.

Conclusion

THE human body is one of the most beautiful, graceful, intelligent and wonderful creation of God. It is both active and passive, soft and violent, rational and emotional. It can experience the divine while it can also become the devil incarnate. It is through the human body that man achieves and experiences. The Absolute descended on the Earth in a human form and the aspirant by absolute surrender attains Him. The human body is mysterious and unfathomable. It has morphogenetic fields of unwrapped energy. The human body is the abode of Śiva and Śakti.

The aspiration for higher things led to a continued search for the Absolute. This also led to the development of various systems of education or *sādhanā* : Yoga, Tantra, *Saṅgīta*. The ultimate object being relinquishment or liberation (*mokṣa*) as the final stage. The end of this discipline is variously known as self-realization (*siddhi*), emancipation (*mukti*), enlightenment (*jñāna*), liberation (*mokṣa/nirvāṇa*) and bliss (*ānanda*). In substance it is the absolute integration of the human personality, freed from the limitations of attachment or fear. Whether in religion or in art, it is a continuous process of discovery — a search for harmony and balance and a realization of the inner or the ultimate truth. The quest for the Absolute is predominant in Indian culture. In fact, as we have seen earlier, the motives and the ideals of all traditional Indian arts is the essence of "sacredness." Coomaraswamy rightly observes that India is the epitome of traditional cultures which were essentially spiritual. The very thought carries within itself the idea of metamorphosis, which involves the process of transformation of form, function and behaviour. The formulation of the theory of art is in fact, a result of the understanding of the philosophy of the mystery of creation.

> The making of the work of art is a ritual. Its magic is active in the form. By performing the rites of art, the craftsman transforms himself and his substance. Form, performance and transformation are simultaneous, inseparable aspects of Indian art. They inhere in its creation and produce their effect in its concrete shape. . . . With open eyes, the Indian artist sees the world around him. With closed eyes he sees the world within him. His vision is direct and twofold.[1]

The Indian approach to art is a holistic approach and like all other spiritual activity there is a discipline and a ritual, which explains the use of highly abstract imagery and symbolism of objects and myths, of lines vertical, horizontal, curved, dots and circles. This man-universe relationship was also discovered in the art and science of *saṅgīta*, which included music and dance.

Nāṭya-Śāstra refers to the generic relation and significance of all arts and yet specifies their autonomous status.[2] Though variously described with a similarity of purpose and an eagerness to control the cosmic forces through various methods of integration and interpretation,

1. Stella Kramrisch, *Exploring India's Sacred Art*, Philadelphia, 1983, pp. 27-28, also see p. 62, wherein she says "Creative work has the Sanctions of a sacrament."

2. Bharata Muni, *Nāṭya-Śāstra*, 1.107, 1.113-117, pp. 133-36, with commentaries *Abhinavabhāratī*, *Madhusūdanī* and *Bālakrīḍā*, infra. Also see Kumbha, Maharāṇa, *Saṅgītarāja*, vol. I, p. 94, infra, wherein the purport of a quotation from the Yājñavalkya seems to be that witnessing a dance performance is specially efficacious in the apprehension of the all pervading unity in the diversity of names and forms (*nāma and rūpa*) in our common experience. This metaphysical apprehension can definitely lead to *nivṛtti* just as the pursuit of *trivarga* leads to *pravṛtti*.

through the manifestation of *Nāda* as sound energy or in terms of space division and time sequence, the Indian arts of music and dance (*saṅgīta*) go even beyond time and space. In other words, they become a medium for the soul to transcend into the unmanifest space, the *cidākāśa*, in which time is inherent. Space symbolizing the static principle and time symbolizing the kinetic principle, are the two principles of Nature and thus also of the Indian arts of music and dance. Prem Lata Sharma says,

> Philosophically there are two principles in Nature : One which is mobile and the other is immobile. All arts refer to the former as the subject and come near the sphere of *Nāṭya*, a term which is derived from the root *naṭ* meaning "अवस्पन्दम" i.e., all that moves or vibrates. Thus, according to the Indian Śāstras, music is one of many arts which deals with objects, which are subject to motion or vibration and which collectively bear the generic term *Nāṭya*. All of them can be experienced at graded levels of transcendent super-feeling at the summit whereof is *acintya mahābhāva* (अचिन्त्य महाभाव).[3]

This is the myth of Śiva's cosmic dance of destruction and creation of transformation and rejuvenation, or even of Viṣṇu in *yoga-nidrā*. Both are *ācārya* of *nāṭya*, and dance as a part of *nāṭya* is an auspicious art. Its purpose is self-realization and the *Nāṭya-Śāstra* is ample evidence in itself. In the *Hāravijaya* of Ratnākara, the two concepts are beautifully brought together. The only survivors in the deluge are Śeṣaśāyī and Naṭeśa. The two also come together in the depiction of Cidambaram. In his Rambles of Vedānta, Ayyar says that, "Viṣṇu sleeping on a serpent couch is in the state of *turīyāvasthā* (beyond *jāgrat, svapna* and *suṣupti*). The conch in his hand symbolizes ether, the sky, receptacle of sound. The sound is produced. Like the drum of Naṭarāja, the conch of Śeṣaśāyī produces sound. The sound

3. Prem Lata Sharma, *Indian Aesthetics and Musicology* (*The Art and Science of Indian Music*), p. 33, infra.

is a symbol of creation. . . ." He further draws parallels between the flaming *cakra* of Viṣṇu and the flame in the hand of Naṭarāja, they are both symbols of creation, destruction, transformation and rejuvenation. Thus, it is a symbol of birth and death. The *māyā* of Viṣṇu, the very charm of life which revolves in an eddy is comparable to the *kuṇḍalinī,* (the snake that curls in circles) and suggestive of the perennial cycle of birth and death, is compared to the snakes encircling the hand, earlobe, matted locks, wrist ankles and waist of Śiva as Naṭarāja. The *gadā* of Viṣṇu symbolizes the power to protect the weak and destroy the evil. This finds a parallel in the hand of Śiva in *abhaya-mudrā*. The lotus in the hand of Viṣṇu is a symbol of *rasa* (water), beauty, charm and good. This finds a parallel in the Gaṅgā, the pure celestial river, issuing out of the *jaṭā*s of Śiva, with the moon in its vicinity appearing almost like a lotus sprung out of the water. Śiva crushes ignorance and evil under his foot when he dances, while Viṣṇu destroys the monsters Madhu and Kaiṭabha, symbols of ignorance and destruction, even as he is still recumbent. In fact, the inspiration for *vṛtti*s in *nāṭya* was drawn by Brahmā from this very episode. Also while Śiva's *tāṇḍava* shakes the heaven's, the earth and the celestial spheres, Viṣṇu measures the three worlds as Trivikrama. Translated in terms of space and time, Śiva symbolizes the vertical meridian while Viṣṇu symbolizes the horizontal time. They are both symbols of the static and kinetic energy, the synthesis of which is dance.[4]

The theory of *guṇa*s in religion, philosophy and *Āyurveda* is also intimately connected with the symbolism of space direction.[5] *Sattva* is the ascending tendency towards

4. C. Sivaramamurti, *Nataraja in Art Thought and Literature, op. cit.*, pp. 36-37, 261, 329.

5. Alice Boner, *Principles of Composition in Hindu Sculpture*, p. 246, infra.

consciousness, light and truth; *Rajas* is the expanding dynamic tendency of power and *Tamas* is the descending tendency weighed down by inertia, darkness and ignorance. The five elements or *tattva*s also correspond to the space directions and the *guṇa*s. Fire (*anala*) is ascending and so it corresponds to *sattva;* Earth (*pṛthvī*) and water (*apa*) are descending and so correspond with *tamoguṇa;* Air (*vāyu*) is expanding and so it corresponds with *rajoguṇa;* Ether (*ākāśa*) lies at the undifferentiated centre and is all-pervading and omnipresent and on the level of manifestation it correspond to *cidākāśa* or to *bindu* on the spiritual level.

The human body is also composed of these five elements (according to some scholars the sixth is the unmanifest *Brahman* or the transcendent Reality), and thus constitutes the *Puruṣa*. Of that *Puruṣa,* the earth forms the image, water forms the liquid, fire constitutes the heat, air acts as the vital breath, hollowness is caused by ether, and *Brahman* is the inner soul. The properties of *ākāśa* (ether) are sound, the sense of hearing, porosity and differentiation, evolution of the veins, ligaments, etc., into their characteristic species (*viviktatā*). The properties of *vāyu* (ether) are touch, the skin, all functional activities of the organism, throbbing of the whole body (*spandana*) and lightness. The properties of *teja* (fire or heat) are form, the eyes, the colours, heat, illumination digestion, anger, generation of instantaneous energy and valour. The properties of *apa* (water or liquid) are taste, the tongue, fluidity, heaviness, coldness, oleaginous and semen. The properties or modifications of *pṛthvī* (the earth matter or solid) are smell, the nose, embodiment of heaviness.[6]

6. *Saṅgītaratanākara*, vol. I, pp. 58-59, tr. Prem Lata Sharma and Shringy, infra. Also see Prem Lata Sharma, *Indian Aesthetics and Musicology* (*The Art and Science of Indian Music*), pp. 58-59, infra, where is also explained that *guṇa* is one of the basic concepts of Indian poetics and it has a special →

The art of dancing exploits the human body to the utmost and as such it would be in line to deduce that these fundamental conceptions were also common to or formed the basis of the compositional movements in dance — in our case *Kathaka*. I have already discussed the inter-relatedness of the Indian arts. The principles of composition which control and govern the logics of other arts are thus common to the principles which constitute the basic framework of *Kathaka* Dance. The profound symbolism, with which the dance is composed, thus corresponds to those very irreversible cosmic principles so explicitly exemplified in the *Tantra-Śāstra* : the dot (*bindu*), the line (*rekhā*), the circle (*maṇḍala*) and the triangle (*trikoṇa*), which though strictly mathematical and geometrical, in the recesses of time conjured up an esoteric significance as well. Symbolism was thus a method, developed by the *sādhaka*s or the *ṛṣi*s of ancient India, to manifest the macrocosm in the microcosm. *Kathaka* in its own unique way has articulated the symbolism in its imagery of movements, as performed in the various compositions, foot-work and *abhinaya*. The tradition of transmitting the esoteric doctrines/knowledge on the lines of the *guru-śiṣya paramparā* in *Kathaka* is still visible in the ritual of the *gaṇḍā-bāndhanā*, i.e., tying of the sacred thread/knot around the wrist of the *śiṣya* by the *guru* and the *śiṣya* thus joining the *guru*'s family as a member. The symbolism of this ritual is that the thread represents the umbilical chord which joins the *śiṣya* to the *guru*, the student thus becoming a custodial of that tradition. Interestingly the thread in the Hindī language is called the *nārā* and the ritual is also referred to as the *nārā-bāndhanā*. *Nārā* in the Hindī language also means the umbilical cord. Thus, the traditional artist was

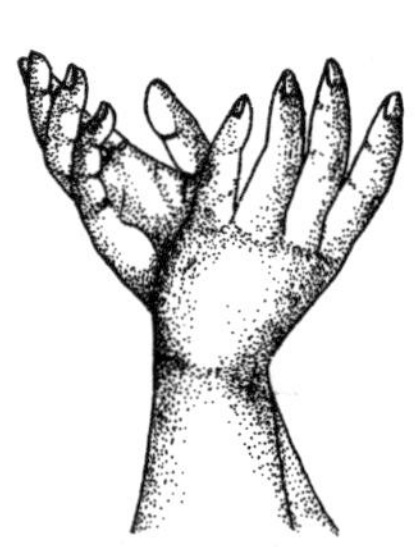

→ philosophical significance as well. It connotes "प्रमाया असाधारणकारणम्" which means an uncommon cause of pure and absolute knowledge. It may also be taken as *rasa*.

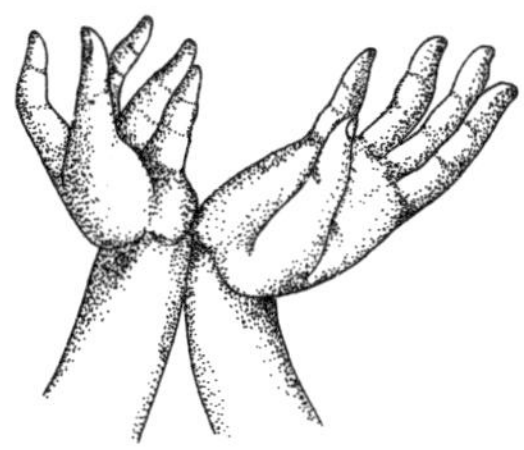

dedicated to the realization of a metaphysical or religious idea. The rules according to which he worked were derived from the spiritual conceptions inherited as part of a vibrant tradition where the effort or the thrust was towards completion, and fulfilment. Thus, every part of a movement whether in a line or a circle or even a curve, carried within itself the power of suggestion, the possibility or the potentiality of expansion indicative of infinity or projection into space. If the straight line suggested a part of a greater line which was invisible, the curving line suggested symbolically, the collecting of movements and rounding them up, just as its gradual increase or decrease, which resulted in a spiral symbolizing the process of contraction or expansion or involution and evolution. The movements through the various modes of repetition and pauses have either an echo or a prolongation in the relief-field. "To create an effective movement at least two opposite stresses have to come into operation, or it has to be brought to life by the contrast of static elements."[7] The artists of ancient India were seers, fully aware of the meanings and significance of movements and their manifestations in various forms of art.

Śiva with his Śakti is represented in Ardhanārīśvara while the Śakti of Viṣṇu is portrayed as Lakṣmī sitting at his feet, while he sleeps on the Śeṣāśāyī; Viṣṇu may also be seen as Ardhanārī Viṣṇu referred to as Viṣṇu-Kamalājā; the Śakti of Kṛṣṇa, Rādhā, is always portrayed in movements/efforts which will culminate in her union with Kṛṣṇa. They are the eternal lovers. It is in fact the union or *yoga* of the *puruṣa* with the *prakṛti* which forms the main thrust of Tantra. In fact, both Yoga and Tantra are basically methods of understanding the Indian Principle, for it is only through inward contemplation that man acquires the

7. Alice Boner, *Principles of Composition in Hindu Sculpture*, p. 49, *op. cit.*

power to remake his vision, both of himself and of the world. It is in this process that the human body becomes the sanctum wherein dwells the Lord. In dance, the movements of the dancer are perhaps, a visualization of the power of the divine presence. The *āsanas* and the *mudrās* which are common to the systems of Yoga, Tantra and *Nṛtta* are in fact configurations of certain forces and moods for releasing and realizing particular forces and energies. They also produce physiological diagrams.

It is also amply clear that the Form in *saṅgīta* is only a manifestation of *nāda* and dance is a visible manifestation of that *nāda*. It is giving an image to that sound which is both meaningless and meaningful. This is a cosmic conception and a transcendent metaphysical vision. The *nāda* in dance is exploited at two levels : the level of the dancer when it comes out or manifests as *light* in the various movements and postures, or at the level of the accompanists who sing and play for the dancer. The musical sound which accompanies a dance performance and which is produced from the throat of the singer or the sound which is produced from the instruments or even the sound which is being created by the movements of the dancer though apparently abstract and inaudible when formulated and performed portray in essence, a Life force which results in *Ānanda*.

According to Ratnākara, there is an ancient belief that the musical orchestra helps to remove *viṣa* or poison. Sivaramamurti states :

> Śiva as the greatest of physicians, *bhiśaktama* among the *bhiśajas*, the greatest among the physicians, as the Veda would have it, is the great God who swallowed the deadliest poison, *kālakūṭa*. Naturally Śiva's orchestra of *vīṇā*, *veṇu* and *mṛdaṅga*, can be held to be consecrated by *mantra* and thus remove all *viṣa* or poison. The general belief that

consecrated musical instruments remove poison is thus voiced by Ratnākara : *prastauti mantrakṛta-saṃkṛtirūpaveṇuviṇāravopi viṣamasya viṣasya nāśam* (*Hāravijaya*, 16.9).[8]

It would do well to remember that the *ghuṅghrūs* (ankle bells) in dance are also worshipped by the dancer as part of a ritual before they are worn by the dancer on his feet. *Nṛtta*, thus, as the third *tattva* of *saṅgīta* stands amply validated. Śiva is a great dancer, He is Naṭarāja and Nṛtyaśīla. His fondness for orchestra, music and dance is qualified by the epithet Vādyanṛtyaprīya; He is the foremost amongst musicians and artists and is consecrated with the epithet Śilpīśa. It was only the *ḍamaru* (kettledrum) of Śiva — which revealed the fourteen *sūtras* to Pāṇini with which he could later create the *Aṣṭādhyāyī*, which was not just a codification of the grammar of language, but a ladder to celestial abode.[9]

Through the work of successive generations the outer form of *Kathaka* has evolved, though the spiritual content seems to have been missed out at various points of history, or even reinterpreted with the changes in the society. The interpretation and analysis of some of the basic movements of *Kathaka*, as in use today, is thus part of a whole and so is tentative. The spectrum of symbolism is so wide, their referential area so broad, that it can be envisaged from various levels of vision. The work however has revealed an abstract and abstruce symbolism corresponding to an esoteric practice in which images and diagrams represent a kind of a fundamental *yantra*. In dance, the enclosing of the sacred space for a performance thus corresponds to the

---

8. C. Sivaramamurti, *Nataraja in Art Thought and Literature*, p. 7, infra.
9. C. Sivaramamurti, *Nataraja in Art Thought and Literature*, p. 24.

formation of a *yantra*. Besides, the various positions of the hands and the feet of the dancer very clearly exhibit the formation of triangles, lines, dots and circles, or *yantra* formations. This *yantra* is made powerful by the utterance of the *mantra*. The mnemonic syllables used in *Kathaka*, whether uttered at the level of the *vaikharī* or even in the movements of the dancer in space (though the sound is not audible), or by the feet of the dancer striking the ground have revealed the extraordinary power vibrating in them. How else can one explain the phenomenon in which an audience of thousands sits glued, as if mesmerized, when a *Kathaka*, dancer does *paḍhanta* or performs *tukaḍā* or *tatkāra* or enacts *abhinaya*, creating patterns or images of sound. It is the ultimate conversion of sound energy into light energy which manifests in the movements of the dancer, thus taking a visible form. The word *camaka* (shine), so often used for good, "class" performances of *Kathaka*, is in fact a process of conversion and manifestation of sound energy into light energy as explained in the science of Physics. Thus, the mnemonic syllables or the sounds symbolize the *mantra*s which vibrate the *yantra*s and this is the system of Tantra. In fact, the tāntric rituals formed the basis of many philosophical, religious and saṅgītic systems of Indian culture, because of their effectiveness in awakening the *kuṇḍalinī*, the vital force, and raising it up from the *mūlādhāra*, through the various *cakra*s, to the *sahasarāra*, the point of eternal Bliss. It is only then that artistic creations acquire magical effects and dimensions.

Like all studies, this work is not the final word. It is another step towards a deeper and a more philosophic interpretation and understanding of an art form which appears embedded with the philosophic, religious, cultural, social and artistic values and interpretations — all inter-linked at various levels to give a distinctness to *Kathaka*. The movements of the dancer in space and time is not a

new concept to the science and art of dance, which like all Indian arts transcends time, yet the study is an attempt towards re-visualizing ideas and thoughts which as part of the great Indian tradition, a legacy of Indian culture, have still stood the test of time. The Indian dancer, dancing bare-footed is not just a coincidence, it is a beautiful, effective and therapeutic method of charging the body through direct contact with the magnetic field of the earth. *Kathaka* as an art form, is an expression of the meaning of life in perceptual terms and it is only the artist, who as a *sādhaka*, acquires the caliber to breathe into disembodied abstract principles the breath of life and the warmth of humanity.

Visuals

Pl. 1. Śrī Yantra,
seventeenth-eighteenth century, south India.

Pl. 2. Rāma Yantra,
seventeenth-eighteenth century, south India.

Pl. 3. Naṭarāja Śiva, Tenth century AD, Coḷa, Tanjore.

Pl. 4. Viṣṇu as Trivikrama, ninth century AD, Elora, showing Time division.

Pl. 5. Viṣṇu as Trivikrama, ninth century AD, Elora, showing Space division.

Pl. 6. Śeṣaśāyī Viṣṇu, fifth century AD, Deogarh, Jhansi.

Pl. 7. Dancing Ardhanārīśvara (Bronze), eighteenth century AD, Tanjore.

Pl. 8. Rāgini Khambāvati, Rāgini of Śrī Rāga, eighteenth century AD, Rajasthani.

Pl. 9. Rāga Basanta, seventeenth century AD, Malwa.

Pl. 10. Dancing Vārāhī, ninth-tenth century AD, Varanasi Province.

Pl. 11. Veśa Parivartana, Leela Hāva, seventeenth century AD, Mewar.

Pl. 12. Veśa Parivartana, Leela Hāva, eighteenth century AD, Bundi.

Pl. 13. Veśa Parivartana, Leela Hāva, eighteenth century AD, Guler Kangra.

Pl. 14. The author in the first stance of Kathaka, Standing in *samapāda*, *samabhaṅga* and holding a *samadaṁśa hasta mudrā*. See the triangle formation.

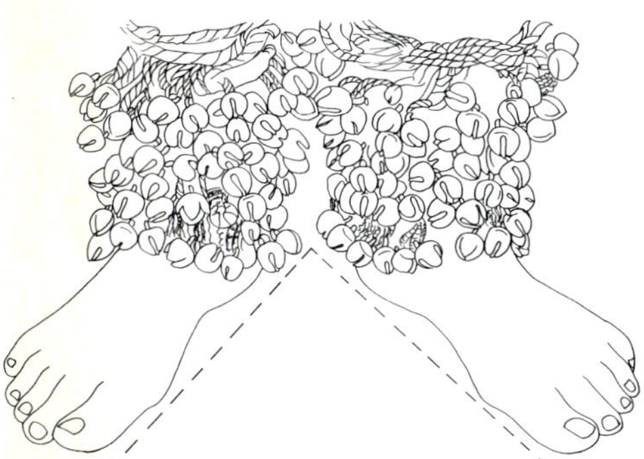

Pl. 15. The author standing in *samapāda*, see the triangle formation.

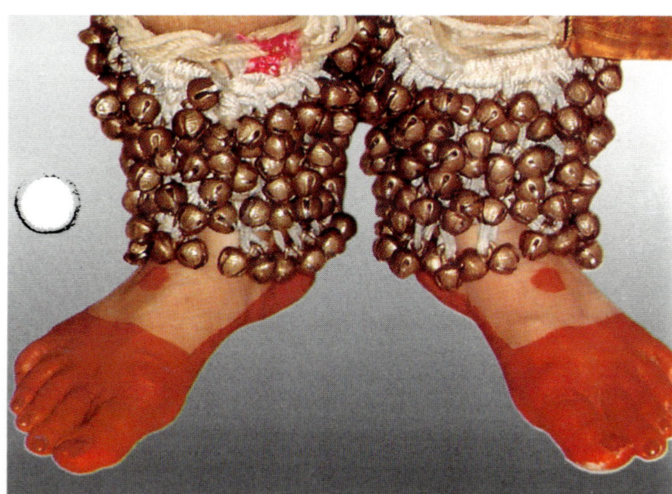

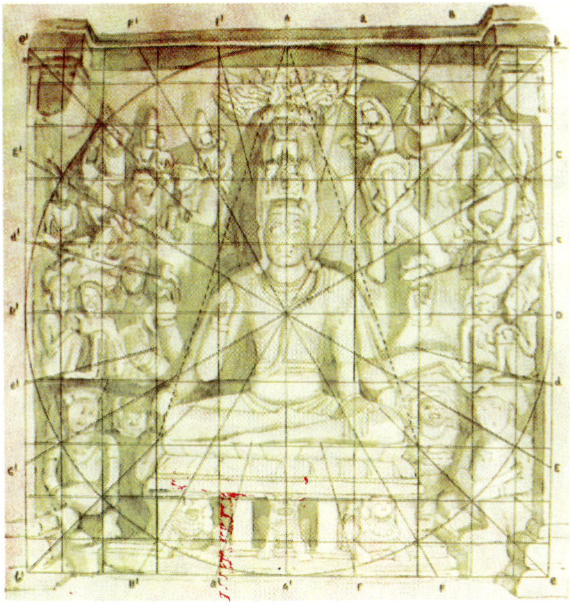

Pl. 16. Śiva the yogi, (showing Space division).

Pl. 17. Śiva the yogi, (showing Time division).

Pl. 18. Suddhama Sabhā (Chudāmaho Utsava), second century BC, Bharhut, central India.

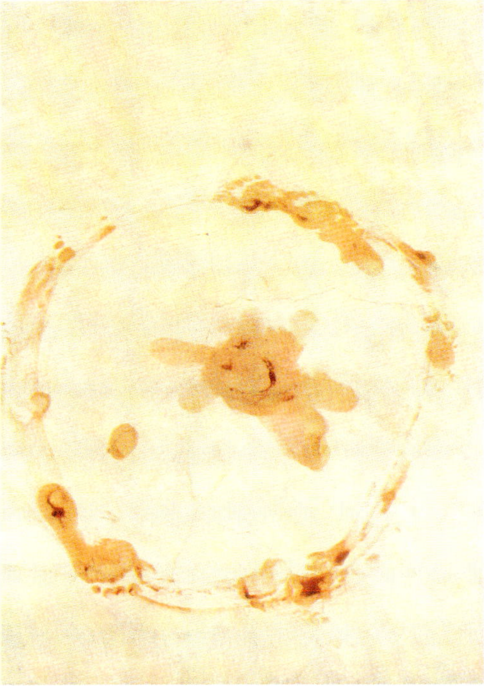

Pl. 19. Circle formation while dancing, by the author.

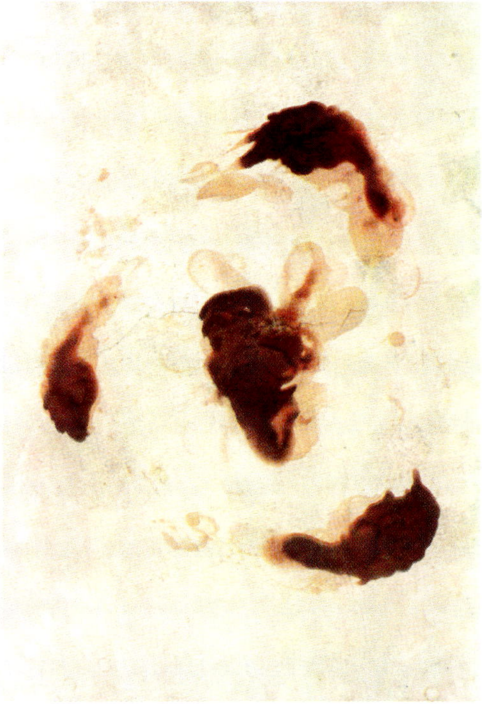

Pl. 20. Triangle formation while dancing, by the author.

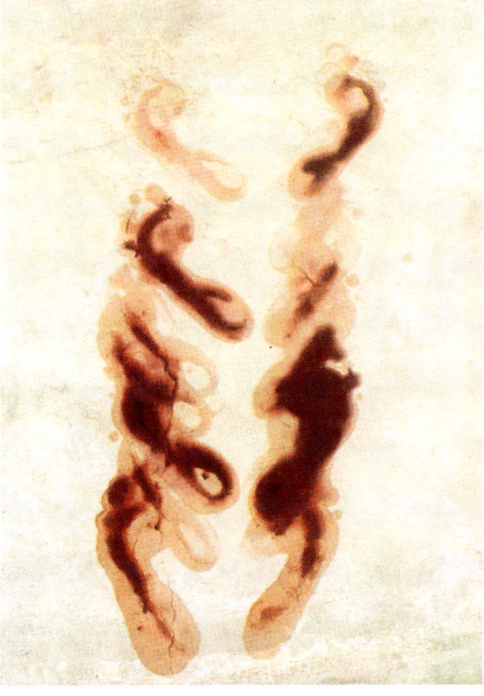

Pl. 21. Line formation while dancing, by the author.

Pl. 22. The author taking a *cakkara*.

Pl. 23. The *Rāsamaṇḍala*, eighteenth century AD, Nāthdvara.

Pl. 24. The author performing the movement of "*tram*".

Pl. 25. Movement of "*tram*".

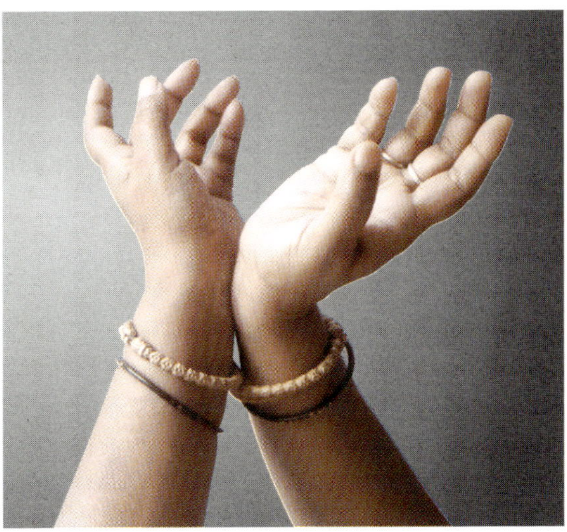

Pl. 26. Movement of "*tram*".

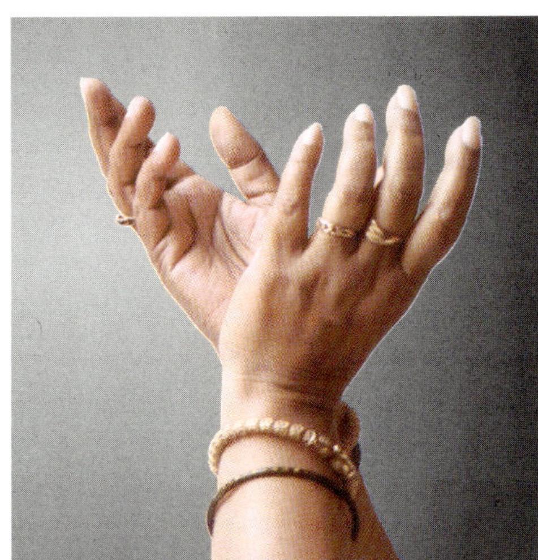

Pl. 27. Movement of "*tram*".

Pl. 28. The author in one of the popular stances of Kathaka, The feet crossed in a *svāstika*.

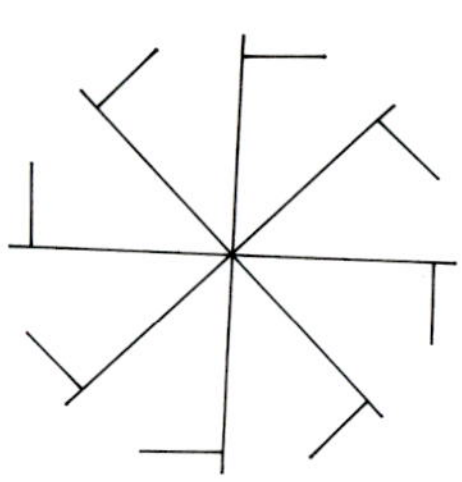

Pl. 29. The author standing in the *svāstika* of the feet.

Pl. 30. The author performing the finishing of a composition. The diaganal line brings force in the movement.

Pl. 31. The author performing *abhinaya*, enacting *gagari*.

Pl. 32. Adoration of Buddhas bowl by the celestials, second century AD, showing the spiral formation.

Pl. 33. Holi, eighteenth century AD, Guler, Showing the pyramid formation (courtesy: Bharat Kala Bhavan, Varanasi).

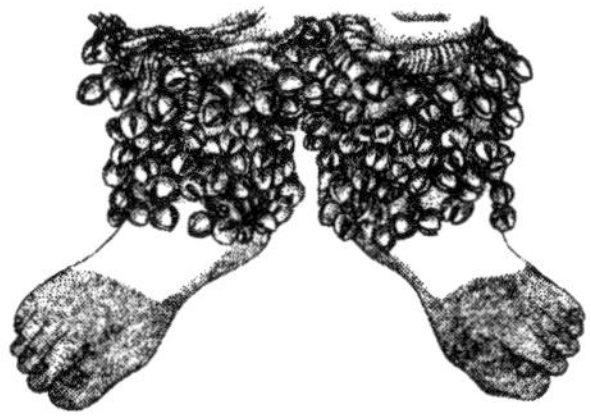

Glossary

Abhaya-mudrā	: A *mudrā* of the hand expressing fearlessness.
Abhidhānavāna	: Meaningful.
Abhinaya	: Acting.
Abhyudaya	: Upliftment.
Abinaya	: Acting
Ācārya	: A senior person who is knowledgeable; a senior *guru*.
Āhārya	: One kind of *abhinaya*. Also see *āṅgika*.
Āhata nāda	: See *nāda*.
Aṁśa	: Partial manifestation of the whole.
Ākāra	: Shape.
Ākāśa	: Space.
Alaukika	: Out of the world.
Alpa	: Finite.
Amṛta	: Nectar.
Anāhata nāda	: See *nāda*.
Ānanda	: Bliss.
Ānanda tāṇḍava	: One of the seven kinds of *tāṇḍava* performed by Śiva.
Ānandātamaka	: Full of joy.
Aṅgahāra(s)	: Combination of *karaṇas*, which results in a short dance sequence.
Aṅgas	: Parts which makes the whole.
Āṅgika	: One kind of *abhinaya*, the others being *vācika*, *āhārya* and *sāttvika*.
Anuśāsana	: Discipline.

Artha : Meaning, money.

Arthaśāstra : Derived from the *'sat'* *aṁśa* of *saccidānanda*, as it is initially concerned with gross matter (*mahābhūtas*).

Asaṁyukta : Single hand gestures.

Āsana : Postures or positions of the body.

Aṣṭāṅga yoga : The eight limbs of *yoga*: *yama, niyama, āsana, prāṇāyāma, pratyāhāra, dhāraṇā, dhyāna* and *samādhi*.

Atharvaveda : The fourth Veda, dealing with *rasa*.

Ātmadarśana : Self-realization through introspection.

Ātman : Manifestation of the Brahmā in the human body.

Ātmaśakti : Power of the self.

Avidyā : Ignorance.

Āyudha : Weapon.

Āyurveda : The science which deals with the prolongivity of life.

Baḍaiyā paraṇa : Name of a special *paraṇa* on carpenter.

Bādala paraṇa : Name of a special *paraṇa* on cloud.

*Bandīshale*s : Rhythmic compositions in *saṅgīta*.

Bhāṇḍa : The body.

Bhaṅgī : Position of the torso.

Bhāva : Mood, emotion.

Bhāva(s) : Emotions.

Bhramaraka-s : Circular movements in dance.

Bhū : *Pṛthvī* or the earth (*bhūmi*).

Bhūman : *Parā vāc* beyond the *paśyanti*. It is *saccidānanda* and so immortal.

Bhūmi : See *bhū*.

Bījākṣara : Seed syllable, a form of *mantra*.

Bindu : The point limit beyond which nothing, matter or energy can be contracted or condensed.

Bols : Mnemonic syllables; *vāc-karaṇas*.

Brahmagranthī : The knot of *Brahman*, i.e., the root of life force located at the centre of the body, the navel.

Brahman : The infinite, unborn, imperishable, omnipotent, omniscient, self-luminous, the *paramātman*.

Brahmāṇḍa : Macrocosm.

Brahmarandhra : The doorway to Brahmā in which is situated the *sahasrapatrakamala*.

Buddhi : Related to the mind.

Caitanya : Consciousness, Intelligence.

Camaka : Shine.

Cāris : Movements of the feet.

Caritas : Poetry or songs containing descriptions of the deeds of divinities or kings and nobles.

Chanda : Metre.

Cidākāśa : The unlimited firmament of the mind, consciousness.

Cin-mudrā : See *Samadaṁśa*.

Cit aṁśa : See *sat aṁśa*.

Citrā : See *citra śāstra*.

Citra-Śāstra : The art and science of painting.

Ḍamaru : The kettle-drum.

Dāravī vīṇā : The wooden lute.

Darśana : Philosophy.

Deha : The human body.

Deśī : That which is from the *loka*, not *mārgī*.

Devapūjā : Worship of the *devatās*.

Devatās : Divine beings.

Dhanurveda : An Upaveda derived from the *sat aṁśa* of *saccidānanda*, as it is initially concerned with the gross matter (*mahābhūtas*).

Dhārā : The flow of river or water.

Dhāraṇa : Assimilation.

Dharma : Righteousness.

Dhrupad : A classical style of singing and dancing.

Dhvani : See *nāda*.

Dhyāna : Meditation.

Diśā : Direction, space.

Duḥkha : Sorrow.

Durgā paraṇa : *Paraṇas* composed on various aspects of Durgā.

Gadā : Name of an *āyudha* of Viṣṇu, Hanumān.

Gaja paraṇa : *Paraṇas* composed on the various aspects of Gaṇeśa, as well as the *gaja* or elephant.

Gāna : Singing.

Gāndharva : An Upaveda which deals initially with sound (a *tanmātrā*) which is closer to *nāda*, *Brahman* himself. It is considered to be derived from the *ānanda aṁśa* of *saccidānanda*.

Ghanībhuta Bindu : When all the *tattvas* are present in the totality of manifestation in the *bindu śakti*.

Gīta : Song.

Grahaṇa : Receiving, practise.

Guha : Caverns.

Guṇas : Attributes.

Guru : One who passes on the knowledge to the students.

Haṭha yoga : An aspect of *yoga* which deals with the physical body.

Hāva : The external indications of love in the persona of the lovers.

Hṛdaya : Related to the heart.

Hrīṁkāra : Mystic sound favourite with the Devī.

Iḍā : One of the four principle nerves, situated on the left side of the spinal cord, a symbol of the moon.

Iṣṭa-devatā : Special/favourite deity.

Jagatiya : *Śuśākākṣara*.

Jāgṛta : See *Turīyāvasthā*.

Japa : Repetition of *mantra* on a rosary.

Jarjara : The staff of Viṣṇu.

*Jaṭā*s : Locks.

Jīva : Individual soul.

Jīvātmā : The human soul.

Jhantum : *Śuśākākṣara*s.

Jñāna : Knowledge through meditation, enlightenment.

Jñāna-mudrā : See *Samadaṁśa*.

Jñeya : That which is known.

Kākū : Production of *dhvani* (sound) with tonal inflexion.

Kākū prayoga : Voice culture to produce quality sound.

*Kalā*s : Evolutes of *varṇa*, denotes *prakṛti*, *śakti* and *māyā*: the absolute transcendental power.

Kālī paraṇa : *Paraṇa*s composed on various aspects of *Kālī*.

Kāma : The desire for sex.

Kāya : The physical form.

Kriyā : Action, both voluntary and involuntary.

Kṣudra brahmāṇḍa : Microcosm.

Kuṇḍalinī : The residual power coiled up like a snake around the *svayambhū liṅga*, i.e., the conus medullaries.

*Lakṣaṇa*s : Distinctive features.

Lāsya : Graceful and soft dance associated with Pārvatī — a *sukumāra prayoga*.

Madhyamā : A stage in speech production. Also see *vaikharī*.

Mahābhāva : The highest ideal of aesthetic experience. A term of Vaiṣṇava philosophy.

*Mahābhūta*s : Gross matter.

Mahāvrata : Name of a ceremony in the *Ṛgveda*.

Mana : Related to the *manas*, *antaḥkaraṇa*, also see *puruṣa*.

Maṇḍala : In the tāntric terminology used for a circle.

Maṅgalācaraṇa ślokas : Invocatory verses.

Maṇipūra cakra : Also known as the *nābhi padma*, located around the region of the navel.

Mantra : Words possessing esoteric meaning, they can be meaningful or meaningless.

Mānuṣī vīṇā : The human body.

Mārjali : Name of a ceremony in the *Yajurveda.*

Mātṛkā : Mystic letter also the name of Divine Mother.

Māyā : Illusion.

Mokṣa : Liberation, freedom.

Mṛdaṅga : A percussion instrument, an *avanaddha vādya*.

Mudrā : Positions of the hands and postures of the body.

Mudrita Gamaka : Name of a *gamaka* in vocal music taken with the mouth closed.

Mukti : Emancipation, liberation.

Mūlādhāra : One of the six nerve plexuses situated in the lowest region of the spinal cord where the *kuṇḍalinī* is coiled.

Nābhi : The navel, also see *brahmagranthī.*

Mṛdaṅga : A percussion instrument, an *avanaddha vādya*.

Nāda : The primordial sound. It may be of two forms — *āhata* and *anāhata*. The *anāhata nāda* is believed to be non-conducive to *bhukti* and *mukti,* because of its being too subtle and unmanifest, to hold the loving attention of ordinary human beings.

Nāda-Brahman : *Nāda eva Brahman,* i.e., *nāda* manifested as *Brahman* also known as *śabda Brahman.*

Nada sādhanā : The *svara sādhanā* taken up by *yogī*s as part of spiritual discipline and culture.

Nāda-yoga : *Saṅgīta.*

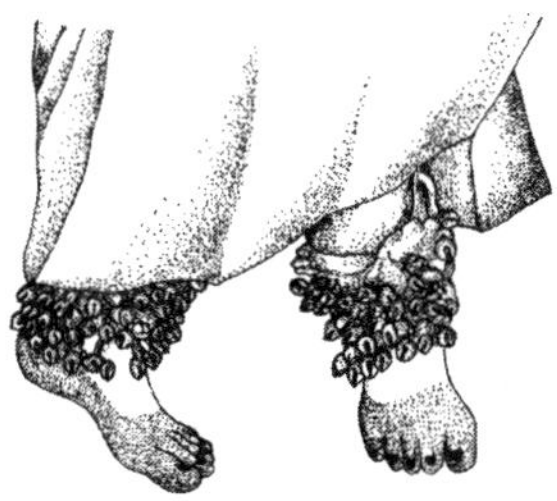

Nadānta	:	A dance of Śiva; where there is cessation of all sound.
Nādātmaka	:	Made of *nāda*, such as Brahmā, Viṣṇu, Maheśa.
Nakṣatras	:	Constellations.
Nāma	:	Name.
Nārā	:	The umbilical chord.
Nartaka Ātmā	:	The dancer is the supreme self.
Nartana	:	*Nṛtta, nṛtya, nātya.*
Nāṭya	:	Also known as the *pañcama* Veda. It includes all the arts and sciences.
Nāṭya maṇḍapa	:	Theatre; Dancing Hall.
Nāyaka-nāyikā bheda	:	Visual representation of the *rāga*s and *rāginī*s.
Niḥśreyas	:	That which is pure and *śreṣṭha.*
Niyama	:	Observance of rules according to the *śāstra*s.
Nṛtta	:	Pure dance.
Nṛtta mūrtis	:	Dancing images.
Nṛtta Śāstra	:	The literature which contains the codification of the principles of *nṛtta* or dance.
Nūpuras	:	Ankle bells, *ghunghroo*s.
Oṁkāra	:	The primordial sound.
Paddhati	:	System of teaching/learning.
Paḍhanta	:	Recitation of the mnemonics in *saṅgita*; also known as *pāṭha.*
Padmanābha	:	An epithet of Viṣṇu.
Pañcakṛtya	:	The five essential acts.
Parā	:	Beyond; also a stage in the production of sound also see *vaikharī.*
Parā-vāc	:	Higher knowledge of sound which expresses itself only at the *mūlādhāra.* It is motionless, without any vibration. It is like a flame of light, unmanifested yet indestructible.
Paramātmā/Paramātman	:	The universal soul. Also see *Brahman.*

Paraṇas : Compositions which are composed of *bols* of *pakhāwaja*.

Paśyanti : One of the stages of the manifestation of *vāc* (speech) related to the *nāda-tattva*.

Paṭākṣaras : See *vāc-karaṇas*.

Pātāla : The underworld.

Pāṭhya : Composed of syllabic or non-syllabic sounds. It is fundamentally concerned with *nāda*. Both the syllabic and non-syllabic sounds are equally powerful in their *vyañyanā śakti* (suggestive power).

Pātra : Vessel.

Paurāṇika : Dealing with the *Purāṇas*.

Piṇḍa : The visible body.

Piṇḍībandha : Group dances in specific formations. Also see *piṇḍī*.

*Piṇḍī*s : A shape, formation. Also see *piṇḍībandha*.

Piṇḍotpatti : The origin from the embryo which corresponds to a lump.

Piṅgalā : An important nerve which along with *iḍā* rises from the *mūlādhara* and ends in the right nostril. Also known as the *sūrya nāḍī*.

Prakāśātmaka : Full of light.

Prakriyā : Process.

Prakṛti : Śakti, the female principle of creation or the primordial energy, identified with Śakti; also Nature.

Pramāṇa : Which is proved or tested.

Prameya : That which is to be proved.

Prāṇa : Life force or the vital force.

Prāṇāyāna : The controlled rhythmic breathing in *yoga*.

Pratimā-pūjana : Worship of idols.

Pravṛtti : Attitude.

Prayoktā(s) : Performers.

Pūjā : Worship.

Pūrṇatā : Completeness.

Puruṣa : Who resides in the eight *purīs*: five motor organs; five sense-organs; four parts of antaḥkaraṇa (viz., *manas, buddhi, ahaṅkāra, citta*); five *prāṇas*; five gross elements, *karma* and *avidyā*. A supraphysical and supramental entity.

Puṣpapuṭa hasta : Name of a *hasta-mudrā*.

Rāga-dhyāna : Visual contemplation of *rāga*s in the form of *nāyaka-nāyikā*s.

Rāgas : A melodic matrix consisting of *svara, tāla* and *pada*, for the ultimate colouring of the mind.

*Rāginī*s : Wives of the *rāga*s.

Rāja yoga : An aspect of *yoga* which deals with the *mānasa*.

Rajas : One of the *guṇa*s which is positive in nature.

Raṅga : Stage.

Raṅga maṇḍapa : *Nāṭya maṇḍapa*.

Raṅga-pūjana : Worship of the stage.

Raṅgmañca : Stage.

Rūpa : Form, appearance.

Rasa : Literally juice. In *Saṅgīta śāstra*, the aesthetic delight. It is *brahmānanda-sahodara*, i.e., delight approximating to universal love.

*Rasiyā*s : Folk songs popular in the Braja-maṇḍala.

Recaka : The rounded movements of the *aṅga*s. It may be of four types: *pāda recaka, kaṭi recaka, hasta recaka* and *grīvā recaka*.

Rekhā : Line, the spinal chord.

Saccidānanda : Truth-consciousness-bliss, Brahmā.

Sādhaka(s) : One who performs *sādhanā*; a real aspirant.

Sādhanā : Spiritual exercise.

Sahaja : Non-dual state.

Sahasrāra : The thousand-lobed centre located in the *brahmarandhra*, i.e., the cerebral aperture.

Sahṛdaya : Connoisseur, a real aesthete.

Śakti : The female energy; the Mother Goddess. Also see *prakṛti*.

Samabhaṅga : Balanced position of the torso.

Samadaṁśa : Position of the hands when the forefinger touches the thumb and the other fingers are opened out also known as *haṁsasya-mudrā* or *jñāna-mudrā* or *cin-mudrā*.

Samapāda : When the feet are placed equally on the ground. A *sthānaka*.

Saṁhāra : Destruction.

Saṁyoga : Union.

Saṁyukta : Combined hand gestures.

Saṅgīta : Music (vocal and instrumental) and dance.

Saṅgīta Śāstra : The literature containing the principles of *prayoga* of the art and science of *saṅgīta*.

Saṅgītika : That which deals with *saṅgīta*.

Sapta-svaras : The seven tones.

Sarasa : Full of *rasa*, delightful, enjoyable.

Śārīrī vīṇā : The human body.

Sarpaśīrṣa hasta : Name of a *hasta-mudrā*.

Sarvatūryaninādi : *Nināda* in the *turīya*.

Śāstras : The literature consisting of doctrines and practises of some discipline generally related to the performance aspect.

Sat aṁśa : One of the three aspects of *saccidānanda*. The others being *cit* and *ānanda*.

Sattva : See *sattva guṇa*.

Sattva guṇa : One of the *guṇa*s which is the highest in order.

Sāttvika : One kind of *abhinaya*. Also see *āṅgika*.

Satya : Truth.

Siddhānta : Principle.

Siddhī : A yogic stage which bestows miraculous powers in the *sādhaka*, who then becomes a *siddha*.

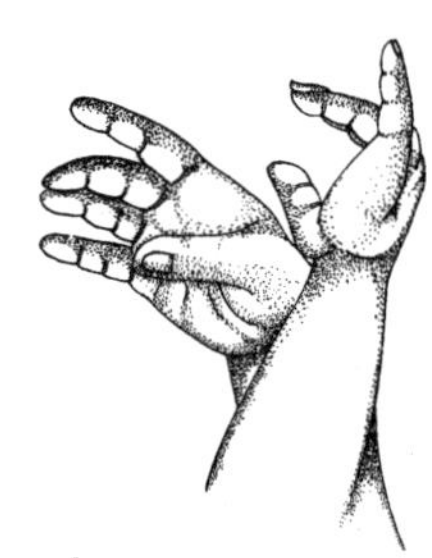

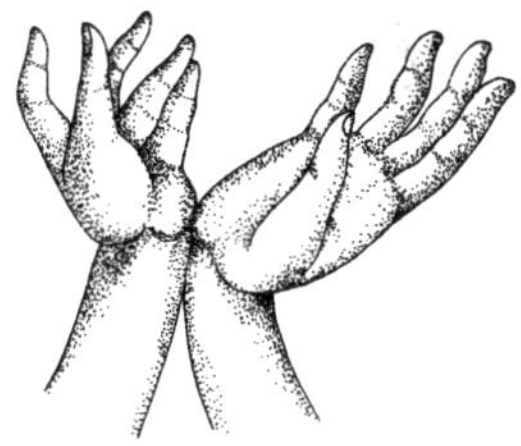

Śilpa : Work of art by man.

Śiva-loka : The abode of Śiva.

Śiva paraṇa : *Paraṇa*s composed on various aspects of Śiva.

Śodhana : Purification.

Somapāna : Drinking of the nectar.

Spandana : Vibration.

Spandanahīna : Wihout any pulsation or vibration.

Sphoṭa-vāda : The theory dealing with sound, its origin and manifestation.

Śṛṅgāra : One of the nine *rasa*s, the erotic.

Sṛṣṭi : Creation.

Śruti : That which is heard — the veda.

Śrutiśākhā : A branch of Veda.

*Sthāna*s : In Tantra the place of manifestation. In dance the standing positions where there is no movement. Also known as *sthānaka*.

Sthāpatya : The art and science of architecture — *Artha-śāstra*.

Sthiti : Preservation.

Stobha : See *stobha kriyā*.

Stobhakriyā : During *pūjā*, when the foot movements accompany the playing of drums and there is no song sung.

Śuddhi : Purification.

Sūkṣma : Subtle.

Sūkta : In Vedic literature, the classification of all the *mantra*s on one subject/topic, such as the *pṛthvi sūkta*.

Sukumāra prayoga : See *lāsya*.

Sulu : A movement performed through *prāṇāyāma* in the starting of a *Kathaka* performance.

*Suśākākṣara*s : *Varṇa*s which are meaningless, also known as *vāc-karaṇa*s.

Suṣumnā : A very important nerve, also known as *Brahma-nāḍī*. It extends from the *mūlādhāra*

	to the *brahmarandhra*. The *kuṇḍalinī* moves upwards through this route.
Suṣupti	: See *Turīyāvasthā*.
Svapna	: See *Turīyāvasthā*.
Svara	: Tone which shines and delights because of the element of *anuraṇana*, i.e., resonance.
Svara sādhanā	: See *nāda-sadhanā*.
Svarvāna	: Tonal.
Svastika	: Sacred symbol represented as 卐
Svātmaparāmarśa	: A state of total unification of mind and soul which results in forgetting of one's purpose, objective and himself.
ta-thei-tata	: Mnemonics of *tatakāra*.
Tāla	: The rhythmic cycle.
Tamas	: One of the *guṇas* which is negative in nature.
Tāṇḍava	: Vigorous and energetic dance associated with Śiva — an *uddhata prayoga*.
Tantra Śāstra	: The literature which contains the codification of the principles governing the science of Tantra.
Tāntric	: That which deals with the science of Tantra.
Tapas	: Penance.
Tatkāra	: Foot-work in *Kathaka*.
Tattva	: Elements, essential principles.
Ṭhumarī	: A semi-classical genre of vocal music, which is infused with *śṛngāra*. A popular item in *Kathaka* recitals.
Tihāī	: Repetition of a set of *bols*, generally at the end of composition.
Titica	: *Suśākākṣara*.
Topa paraṇa	: Name of a special *paraṇa* on cannon.
Trika	: Three, three points of a triangle.
Ṭukaḍās	: Small compositions.
Turīya	: See *turiyāvastha*.

Turīyāvastha	:	Beyond *jāgṛta* (awareness), *svapna* (dream) and *suṣupti* (sleep).
Uccāraṇa	:	Utterance.
Uddhāra	:	Upliftment.
Uddhata prayoga	:	See *tāṇḍava*.
Upāsanā paddhati	:	The system of praying or worshipping.
Vāc	:	Speech, *vāṇī*.
Vāc-karaṇas	:	See *śuśākākṣara*.
Vācika	:	One kind of *abhinaya*, dealing with voice production. Also see *āngika*.
Vādya	:	Instruments.
Vaggeykāra	:	Composer of lyrics/music of songs.
Vaikharī	:	An aspect of speech production, the others being *parā*, *paśyanti* and *madhyamā*.
Vajra	:	Thunder-bolt.
Valitaka	:	*Śuśākākṣara*.
Vāṅgmaya	:	All literature.
Vāṇī	:	See *vāc*.
Varada hasta	:	Name of a *hasta* which bestows blessings.
Varṇa-nāgakṛpārika-bandha	:	A kind of *bandha*.
Varṇas	:	In *yoga* the order of manifestation of *nāda* is from *varaṇa* to *pada* and from *pada* to *vākya*.
Vāstu	:	Architecture.
Vāyu	:	One of the *tattvas*.
Vidhi	:	Right method as advocated in the *śāstras*.
Vidyā	:	Knowledge.
Vīṇā	:	A stringed instrument associated with Sarasvatī.
Viyoga	:	Separation.
Vṛttis	:	Of four kinds: *sātvikī*, *bhāratī*, *ārabhaṭī* and *kaiśikī*.
Vyañjana	:	Suggestion.
Vyāpaka	:	Widespread.

Yajña	: Ritual.
Yantra	: Mystic diagram.
Yoga	: The art and science which deals with the integration of the soul in man first within himself and then between himself and nature.
Yoganidrā	: A yogīc, state in which though there is with-drawal of the outer senses, there is communion with God, the Puruṣottama.
Yogī(s)	: One who has mastered in *yoga*.
Yūpa-s	: Sacrificial posts.

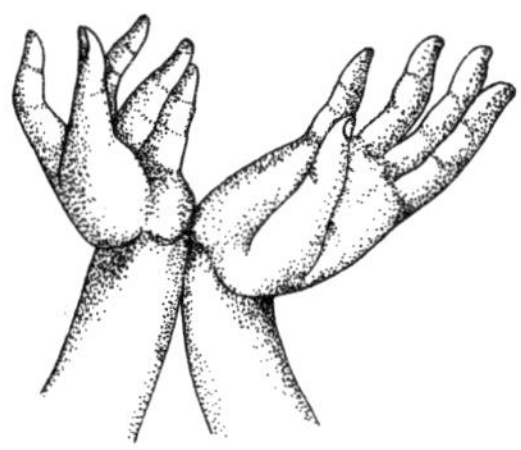

Bibliography

Agarval, V.S., *Śiva Mahadeva : The Great God* (*An exposition of the symbolism of Śiva*), Prithvi Prakashan, Varanasi, 2nd edn., 1984.

Aparājitapṛcchā, A Critical Study (Encyclopaedic Manual on Art and Architecture), Comp. Bhuvandevacarya, ed. Manilal Dubey, Laksmi, Allahabad, 1987.

Ashirvadam, P.D., *Raigarh Darbar*, Agam Kala Prakashan, Delhi, 1990.

Banerji, S.C., *A Brief History of Tantra Literature*, Naya Prokash, Calcutta, 1988

Banerji, S.C., *Fundamentals of Ancient Indian Music and Dance*, L.D. Institute of Indology, Ahmedabad, 1976.

Bharata Muni, *Nāṭya-Śāstra*, vol. I, Manamohan Ghosh, 2nd edn., Granthalaya Pvt. Ltd., Calcutta, 1967.

Bharata Muni, *Nāṭya-Śāstra*, vols. I, 1971; II, 1975; III, 1981, with commentaries *Abhinava- bhāratī, Madhusūdanī* & *Bālakrīḍā*, Banaras Hindu University, Varanasi.

Boner, Alice, *Principles of Composition in Hindu Sculpture, Cave Temple Period*, Leiden, E.J. Brill, Netherlands, 1962.

Bose, D.N., Haldhar, Hiralal, *Tantras* (*Their Philosophy and Occult Secrets*), V.K. Publishing House, New Delhi, 1981.

Chakravarty, H.N., "Mantra and the Significance of Repetitive Sounds," Paper read in the National Seminar on "Dhvani," *Jñāna Pravāha*, Centre for Cultural Studies, Varanasi, 1999.

Chaturvedi, Brajmohan, "Viniyoga, Kalāoṅ kā Saundaryānubhūti me," article in *Saṅgīta Darśan Paricarcā Smārikā*, ed. N. Rajam, Bharatiya Darsanika Anusandhana Parisada and Faculty of Performing Arts, BHU, Varanasi, 1986.

Choudhary, S., *Bhāratiya Saṅgīta Me Tāla Aur Rūpa Vidhāna*, Krishna Brothers, Ajmer, Rajasthan, 1984.

Coomarswamy, A., *Fundamentals of Indian Art*, The Historical Research Documentation Programme, Jaipur, 1985.

Coomarswamy, A., *Rajput Painting*, vol. I, Motilal Banarsidass, Varanasi, 1976.

Douglas, Nik, *Tantra Yoga*, Munshiram Manoharlal, New Delhi, 1971.

Joshi, M.N., *Art and Science in Mansollasa*, New Bharatiya Book Corporation, Delhi, 2003.

Kalātattvakośa, IGNCA, vols. II, 1992; III, 1996; IV, 1999.

Kramrisch, Stella, *Exploring India's Sacred Art*, ed. Barbara Stroller Miller, Philadelphia, 1983.

Kumbhā, Mahārāṇā, "Gitaratnakośa," *Saṅgītarāja*, vol. I, ed. Prem Lata Sharma, Hindu Vishvavidyalaya Sanskrit, Board, Varanasi, 1963.

Mātaṅga Muni, *Bṛhaddeśī*, vol. I-II, ed. Prem Lata Sharma and A.B. Beohar, IGNCA, New Delhi, 1992-94.

Mishra, T.N., *Impact of Tantra in Religion & Art*, D.K. Printworld, New Delhi, 1997.

Mishra, T.N., *Yoga Tantra and Sensuousness in Art*, D.K. Printworld, New Delhi, 2003.

Mukherji, Ajit, *Tantra Art — Its Philosophy and Physics*, Ravi Kumar, New Delhi, 1971.

Mukhopaddhyaya, Govindagopal, "Nāda in Spiritual Culture," Paper read in the Seminar on Dhvani, *Jñāna Pravāha*, Varanasi.

Nandikesvara, *Abhinaya Darpaṇa*, tr. Puru Dadich, Bindu Prakashan, Ujjain, 1988.

Padoux, Andre, *Mantras — What are they* ? Other details missing.

Pandit, M.P., *Studies in the Tantras and the Veda*, Sterling Publishers Pvt. Ltd., New Delhi, 1988.

Randhawa, M.S., *Kangra Paintings on Love*, National Museum, New Delhi, 1962.

Rao, S. Ramachandra, *Yantra*, Sri Satguru Publications, Delhi 1988.

Rawson, Philip, *Tantra*, Thames & Hudson, London, 1973.

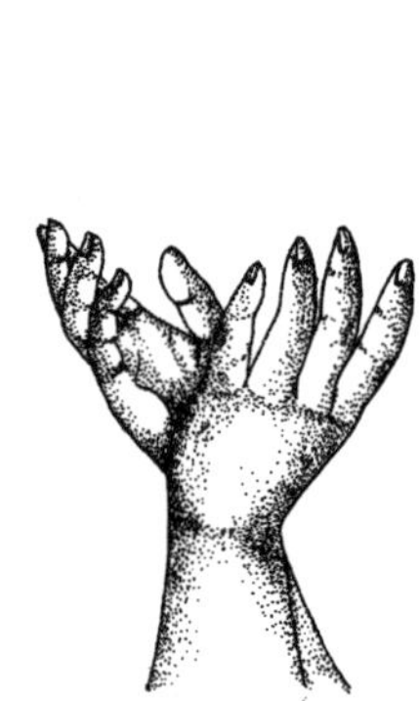

Śārangadeva, *Saṅgītaratnākara*, ed. Pandit S. Subrahamanyam Sastri, vol. IV, The Adyar Library, Madras, 1953.

Śārangadeva, *Saṅgītaratnākara*, Pt. I, Commentary and Translation S. Choudhury, Radha Publications, New Delhi, 2000.

Śārangadeva, *Saṅgītaratnākara*, vols. I, 1999; II, 1989, ed. R.K. Shringy and Prem Lata Sharma, Munshiram Manoharlal, New Delhi.

Śārangadeva, *Saṅgītaratnākara*, vol. IV, Translated by Dr. Kunjunni Raja and Radha Bernier, The Adyar Library and Research Centre, Madras, 1976.

Shah, Priyabala, *Viṣṇudharamottara Purāṇa*, vol. I, Gayakwads Oriental Institute Baroda, 1958.

Sharma, Prem Lata, *Indian Aesthetics and Musicology* (*The Art and Science of Indian Music*), ed., Dr. Urmila Sharma, Amnāya-Prakāśana, Bharata-Nidhi, Varanasi, 2000.

Sharma, Prem Lata, *The Alchemy of Love and Wisdom*, ed. and comp. Dr. Urmila Sharma, Radha Publications, New Delhi, 2002.

Singh, Shanta Serbjeet, ed., *Indian Dance, The Ultimate Metaphor*, Artemisia Ltd., Hong Kong, Bookwish (India) Pvt. Ltd., New Delhi (year not given).

Sinha, B.C., *Hinduism and Symbol Worship*, Agam Kala Prakashan, Delhi, 1983.

Sivaramamurti, C., *Approach to Nature in Indian Art and Thought*, Kanak Pub., New Delhi, 1980.

Sivaramamurti, C., "Dakshiṇamurti Glory of Learning," Lecture delivered at BHU, Varanasi, 1981, manuscript yet to be published.

Sivaramamurti, C., *Nataraja in Art Thought and Literature*, Publications Division, Ministry of Information and Broadcasting, Govt. of India, 1974.

Srivastava, Ranjana, *Kathaka : Its origin and development : A study based on Ancient and Medieval Sculptures and Paintings* [Unpublished].

Sudhi, Padma, *Symbols of Art, Religion and Philosophy*, Intellectual Publishing House, New Delhi, 1988.

Tiwari, M.N., and Kamal Giri, ed., *Kalā*, Journal of Indian Art History Congress, vol. VI.

Vyasa, Veda, *Mahābhārata*, Anuśāsan Parva, pt. II, vol. 17, ed., R.N. Dandekar, Bhandarkar Oriental Research Institute, Poona, 1966.

Vyasa, *Srimada Bhāgawat*, commentary in Hindi by Golokavali Lala Shaligramji Vaishya, Khemraj Srikrishnadasa.

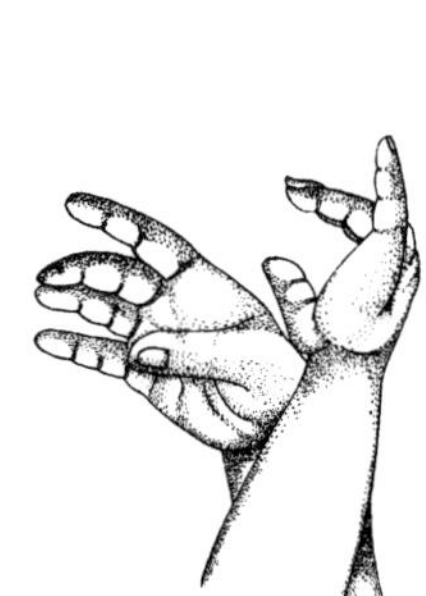

Index

Pl. 1. Pre-historic rock art at Yogīmaṭh Donger of neolithic period, Nuāpāḍā district in Orissa, with author J.P. Singh Deo in 1970.

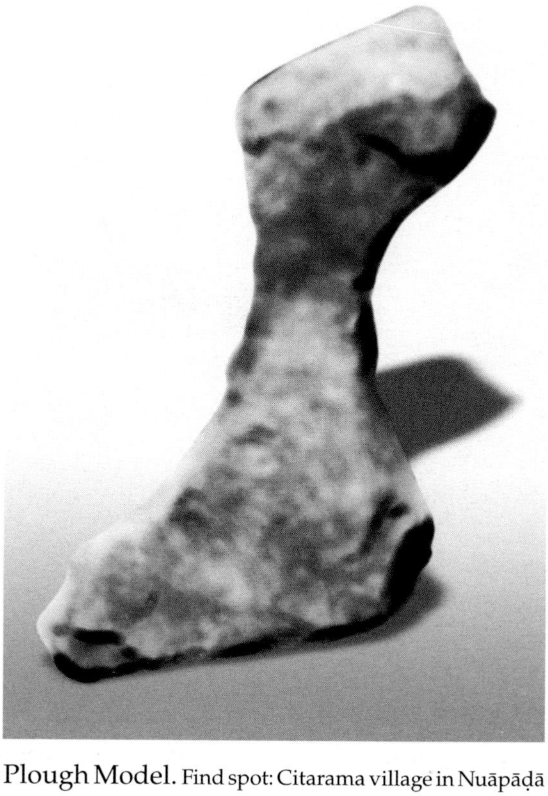

Pl. 2. Stone Plough Model. Find spot: Citarama village in Nuāpāḍā district. *In situ*.

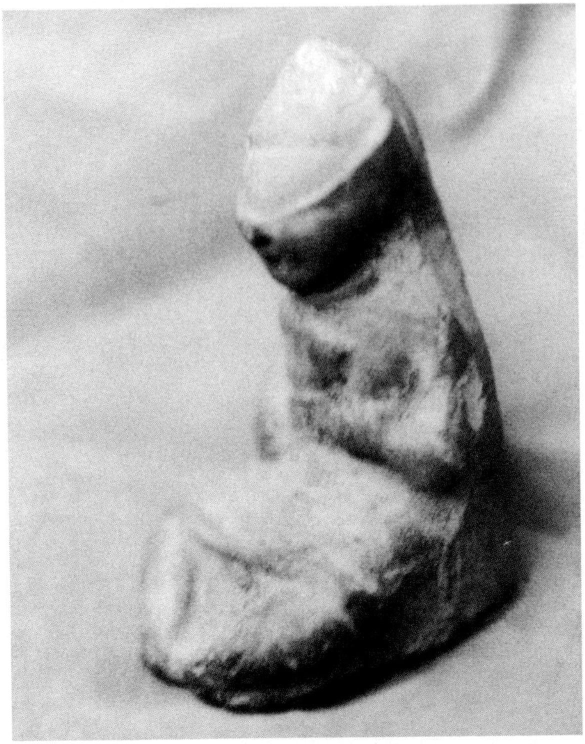

Pl. 3. Steatite figure of a priest, wearing a robe falling from the left shoulder. Find spot: Khariar, Nuāpāḍā district. Kept in private possession of the author. Similar figure has been found at the Indus valley civilization site Gumlā, in Pakistan.

Pl. 4. Śiva-Śakti made in the Āgamic principle with the author J.P. Singh Deo. Find spot: The ruined temple site at Rānīpur-Jharial, Bolaṅgir district, Orissa.

Pl. 5. Discovering a port hole megalithic stone, within the Chaura group of mountains at the Podagarh site, author J.P. Singh Deo with assistant Irfan Mohammad.

Pl. 6. Port stone. Find spot: Podagarh site within the Chaura group of mountains, Nuāpāḍā. Kept in private possession of the author at Khariar.

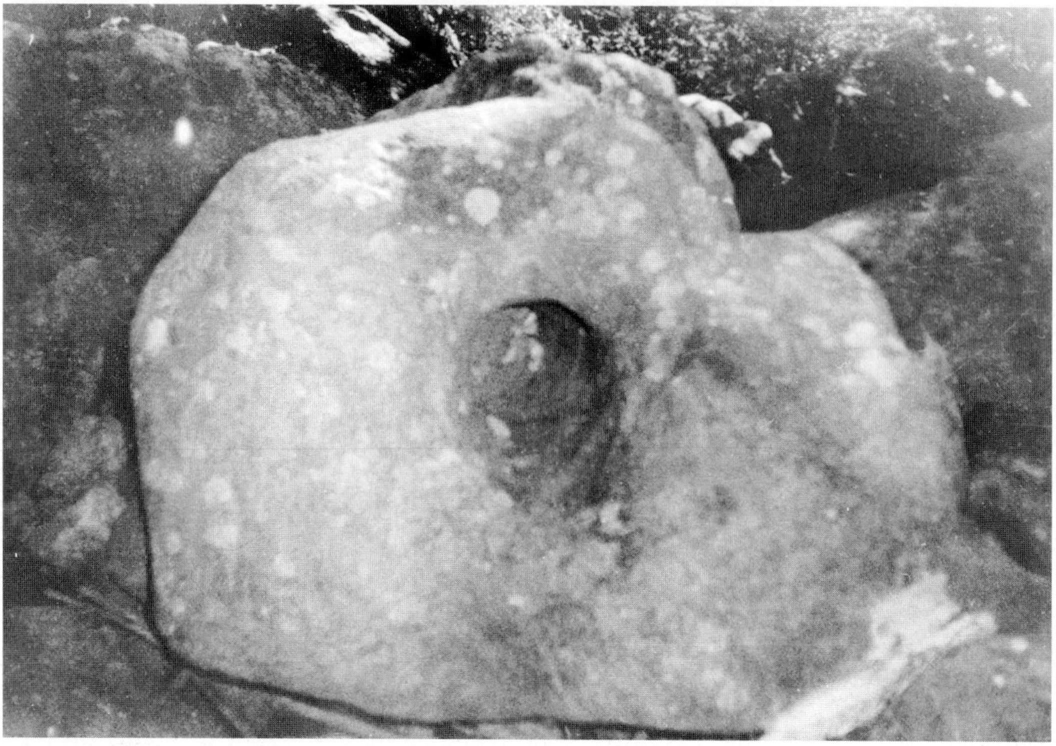

Pl. 7. Port stone. Find spot: The forest around Karlapat in Kālāhāṇḍī district, Orissa. Courtesy: Ranbir Singh of Bhavanipatna.

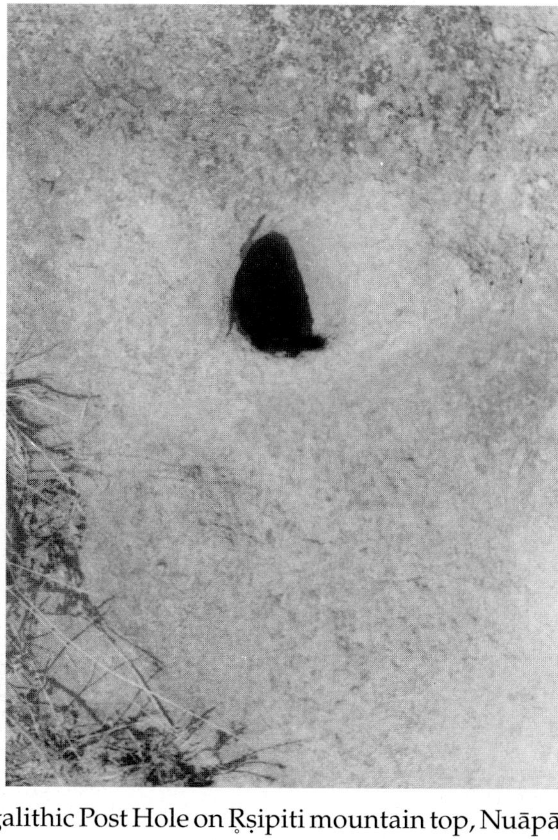

Pl. 8. Megalithic Post Hole on Ṛṣipiti mountain top, Nuāpāḍā district.

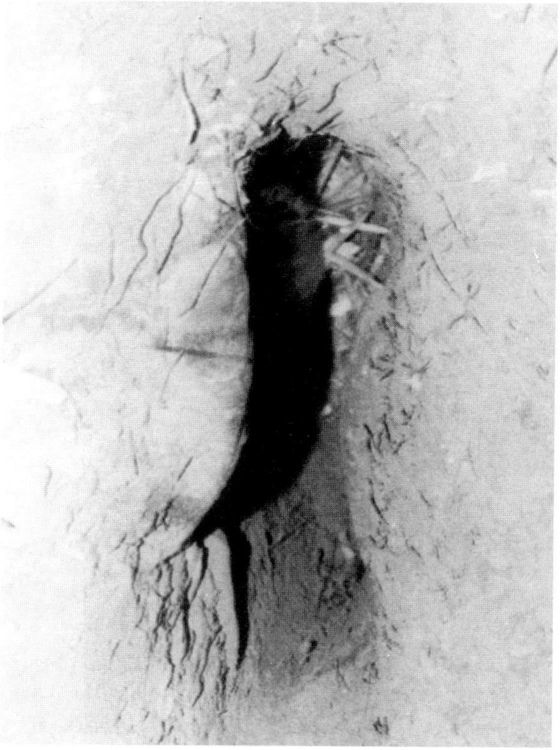

Pl. 9. Naturally formed *yoni* (*yoni gatra*) near the Pātālgaṅgā site of Nuāpāḍā district.

Pl. 10. *Yoni* worshipped as Dwarsani at Sindhekela village, Bolaṅgir district, Orissa.

Pl. 11. *Yoni* of quartzite stone and ferruginous colour. Find spot: The Maraguḍā valley, Nuāpāḍā district. Preserved in private possession of the author at Khariar.

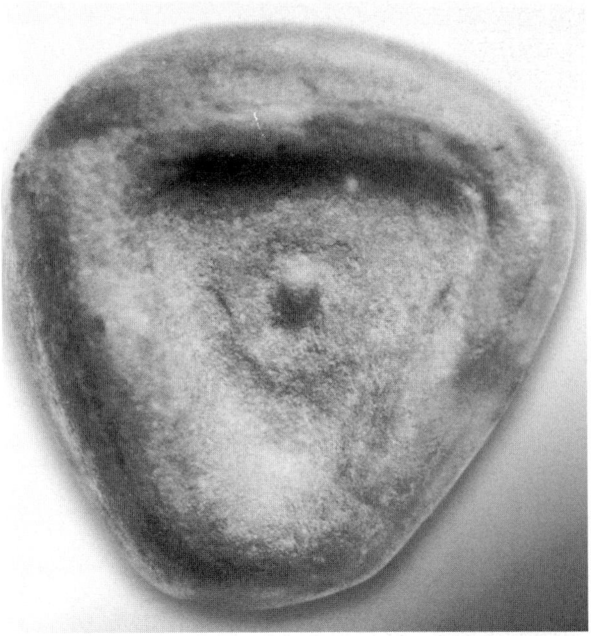

Pl. 12. *Yoni* as Bhairavī Yantra, with a *bindu* (spot) at the centre. According to "Kāma-Kalā-Vilāsa," Tāntric text, this *bindu* is Uḍḍiyāna Pīṭha (site), where Śiva the *guru* (master) loves to abide. Find spot: The river bed of Udanti river in Nuāpāḍā district. Courtesy: Dr. Padma Dandasena. Preserved as household deity in the house of Brusabhanu Naik and Narsingh Naik of Mundapala village, on the left bank of Udanti river, Nuāpāḍā district.

Pl. 13. Stone *yoni* discovered at Dhangritāl village, Nuāpāḍā district. Preserved in private possession of the author.

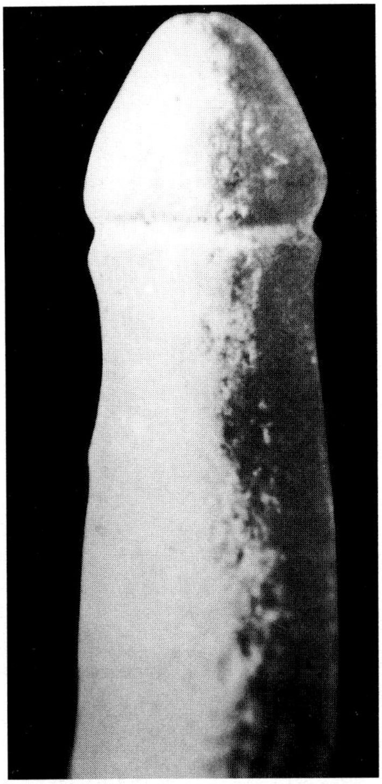

Pl. 14. Stone *liṅga* from Harappā. Courtesy: B.B. Lal. *The Earliest Civilization of South Asia*, Aryan Books International, New Delhi, 1997, photo. L.C.

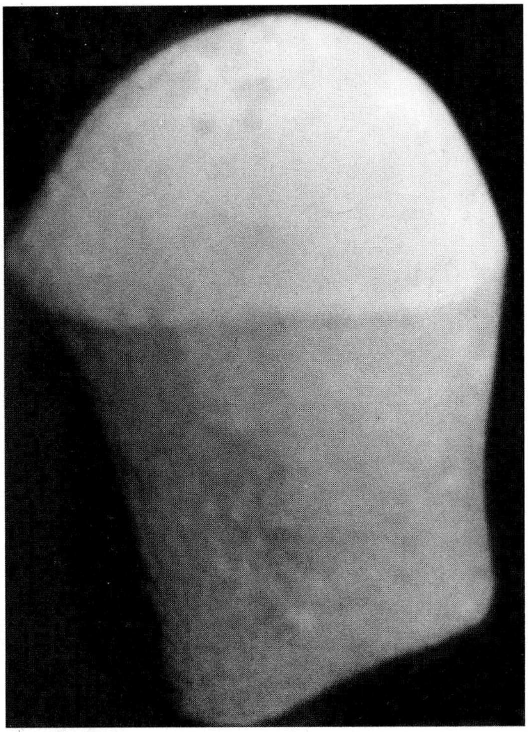

Pl. 15. Broken *liṅga* having similarity with the Harappā findings. Find spot: A high school compound in village Baragāon, to the west of Khariar, Nuāpāḍā district. Preserved in private possession of the author.

Pl. 16. Two circular stone sockets about 25 cm, in diameter. They have components which fit into each other, thereby showing the union of male and female principals. The inner parts are polished. Find spot : Mohangiri, preserved at Manikyapur Museum, Bhavanipatna.

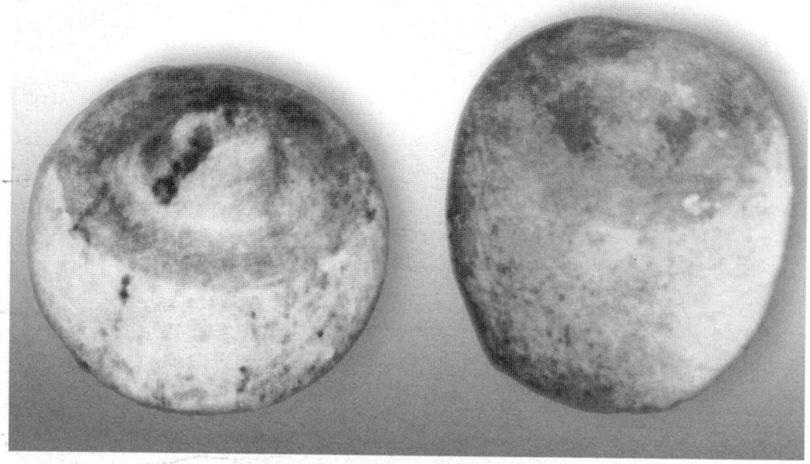

Pl. 17. Exposed stone sockets, showing the female and male principals.

Pl. 18. Stone sockets set. Find spot: Kharligarh site, Bolaṅgir district. Preserved at Manikyapur Museum, Bhavanipatna.

Pl. 19. Exposed stone sockets. Find spot: Kharligarh, Bolaṅgir district.

Pl. 20. Buddha represented at the centre, like the stone sockets findings. Presentation of Rāhula, Cross-Bar from Amarāvatī railing, Archaeological Museum, Amarāvatī, Andhra Pradesh.

Pl. 21. Lajjā Gaurī. Find spot: Kortipadar village area, dist. Nuāpāḍā. Preserved with the author.

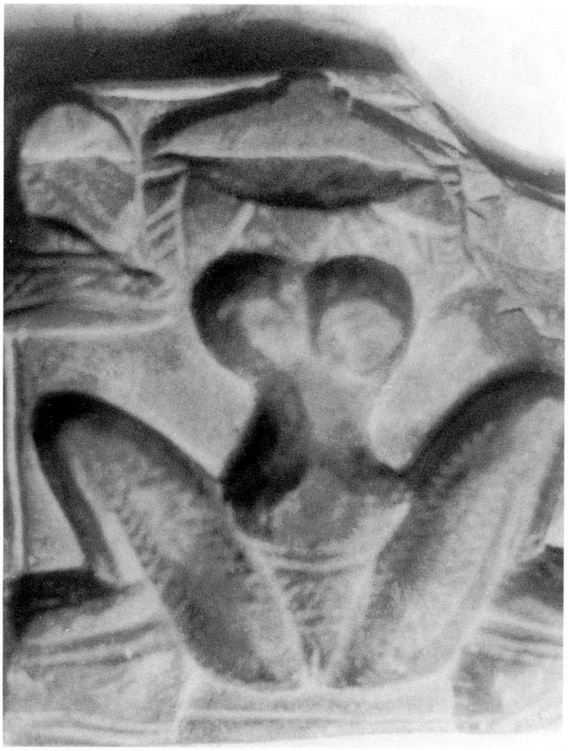

Pl. 22. Lajjā Gaurī. Find spot: The Compound of Panchayat College at Komnā in Nuāpāḍā district. Preserved at "Dr. N.K. Sahu Museum," Sambalpur University, Burla.

Pl. 23. One side of the Terracotta Lajjā Gaurī. Find spot: Mathurā, Uttar Pradesh. Preserved at Victoria & Albert Museum, 177, Mumbai, Maharashtra. Height 3⅘ inches, second century BC.

Pl. 24. The other side of Terracotta Lajjā Gaurī. Find spot: Mathurā. Preserved at Victoria and Albert Museum, 177, Mumbai. Second century BC.

Pl. 25. Eight-handed Naṭarāja Image with Ūrdhvaliṅga. Find spot: Archaeology Museum, Sirpur in Raipur district, Chhattisgarh. Fifth century AD.

Pl. 26. Eight-handed Naṭarāja Image with Ūrdhvaliṅga. Find spot: Āsanapaṭ in Kendujhar district, Orissa. It has inscription of Nāga King. Preserved at Orissa State Museum, Bhubaneśvar. Sixth century AD.

Pl. 27. Composite Tāntric *Haṭha* Yogic figure of Mahākāla and Mahākālī. Find spot: Tala, dist. Bilaspur, Chhattisgarh province. Medieval period.

Pl. 28. Umā-Maheśvar with a headgear found with Lajjā Gaurī in one earthen pot. Find spot: Kortipadar village, Nuāpāḍā district. The headgear shows the influence of the one on an image chiselled on the Śiva-liṅga of Guḍimallam village, Andhra Pradesh. Second century BC.

Pl. 29. Dakṣina Kālī as found in a northern niche of the Kedāreśvara Mahādeva temple at Ichhapur village of Kālāhaṇḍī district, Orissa. Modern construction within the eighteenth-nineteenth century AD.

Pl. 30. Nīlakaṇṭheśvar Śiva temple at Dadpur, Kālāhāṇḍī district. Kalacuri construction, within the twelfth-thirteenth century AD.

Pl. 31. Pātāleśvar Śiva temple of brick construction at Bodhi Komnā, Nuāpāḍā district. Within the seventh-eighth century AD. (Before conservation).

Pl. 32. The view of Pātāleśvara Śiva temple at Bodhi Komnā. (After conservation).

Pl. 33. The view of Pātāleśvara Śiva temple at Bodhi Komnā. (After conservation).

Pl. 34. The view of Pātāleśvara Śiva temple at Bodhi Komnā. (After conservation).

Pl. 35. Different view of the Citāberi Devī temple at Dhobni village, dist. Raipur, Chhattisgarh. Within seventh-eighth century AD.

Pl. 36. Different view of the Citāberi Devī temple at Dhobni village, dist. Raipur, Chhattisgarh. Within seventh-eighth century AD.

Pl. 37. Different view of the Citāberi Devī temple at Dhobni village, dist. Raipur, Chhattisgarh. Within seventh-eighth century AD.

Pl. 38. Different view of the Citāberi Devī temple at Dhobni village, dist. Raipur, Chhattisgarh. Within seventh-eighth century AD.

Pl. 39. Different view of the Citāberi Devī temple at Dhobni village, dist. Raipur, Chhattisgarh. Within seventh-eighth century AD.

Pl. 40. Different view of the Citāberi Devī temple at Dhobni village, dist. Raipur, Chhattisgarh. Within seventh-eighth century AD.

Pl. 41. Different view of the Citāberi Devī temple at Dhobni village, dist. Raipur, Chhattisgarh. Within seventh-eighth century AD.